This Book Belongs To:

....

CHRISTMAS 2009

Christmas with **Southern Living** *2009*

Oxmoor House®

Christmas with **Southern Living** *2009*

Oxmoor House®

ISBN-13: 978-0-8487-3282-0
ISBN-10: 0-8487-3282-0
ISSN: 0747-7791

Printed in the United States of America
First Printing 2009

Oxmoor House, Inc.
VP, Publishing Director: Jim Childs
Executive Editor: Susan Payne Dobbs
Brand Manager: Daniel Fagan
Managing Editor: L. Amanda Owens

Christmas with Southern Living® 2009
Editor: Rebecca Brennan
Foods Editor: Julie Gunter
Project Editor: Vanessa Lynn Rusch
Director, Test Kitchens: Elizabeth Tyler Austin
Assistant Director, Test Kitchens: Julie Christopher
Test Kitchens Professionals: Jane Chambliss,
    Kathleen Royal Phillips, Catherine Crowell Steele,
    Ashley T. Strickland, Deborah Wise
Photography Director: Jim Bathie
Senior Photo Stylist: Kay E. Clarke
Associate Photo Stylist: Katherine Eckert Coyne
Senior Production Manager: Greg A. Amason

Contributors
Designer: Carol Damsky
Copy Editor: Dolores Hydock
Proofreader: Adrienne S. Davis
Indexer: Mary Ann Laurens
Intern: Angela Valente
Food Stylists: Ana Price Kelly, Debby Maugans

To order additional publications, call 1-800-765-6400.

For more books to enrich your life, visit **oxmoorhouse.com**

To search, savor, and share thousands of recipes, visit
myrecipes.com

Cover: Red Velvet Swirl Pound Cake (page 159)
Back Cover: (*clockwise from top left*) Topsy-turvy Tasting Party
(page 53), Mini Muffulettas (page 16), Rustic Yet Refined
(page 21), Chocolate Extreme Cupcakes (page 128)

Contents

YOU'RE INVITED TO MEMORIES IN THE MAKING WITH EVERYTHING FROM A CASUAL OPEN HOUSE TO AN ELF PARTY TO A FAMILY CELEBRATION. GAME PLANS AND STYLISH DECORATING IDEAS ARE INCLUDED IN OUR OFFERINGS THIS SEASON.

Entertaining

HOLIDAY *Open House*

Ring in the holidays with this fantastic menu of flavor combinations your party guests will not soon forget.

menu

Açaí-Berry Mulled Cider

Blood Orange Martinis

Mediterranean Roasted Almonds

Fig, Prosciutto, and Blue Cheese Squares

Caramelized Vidalia Onion Dip

Mini Sun-dried Tomato Cheese Toasts

Mini Muffulettas

Grilled Flat Iron Steak Crostini

Marinated Vegetables

Dark Chocolate-Toffee Brownie Shooters

serves 18 to 24

Up to 1 month ahead:

• Make and freeze Mini Sun-dried Tomato Cheese Toasts.

2 days ahead:

• Make Olive Salad for Mini Muffulettas; assemble muffulettas, if desired.

• Make brownies for Dark Chocolate-Toffee Brownie Shooters.

• Make Mediterranean Roasted Almonds.

• Cook prosciutto for Fig, Prosciutto, and Blue Cheese Squares; cool and store in airtight container in refrigerator.

1 day before party:

• Marinate Flat Iron Steak; prepare Herbed Caper Butter. Cover and chill both recipes.

• Combine ingredients for Blood Orange Martinis; cover and chill.

• Prepare Caramelized Vidalia Onion Dip, but don't bake; cover and chill.

• Prepare Marinated Vegetables; cover and chill.

4 hours before party:

• Assemble Dark Chocolate-Toffee Brownie Shooters; chill.

• Assemble muffulettas, if not already completed.

• Prepare Açaí-Berry Mulled Cider.

• Prepare Fig, Prosciutto, and Blue Cheese Squares.

1 to 2 hours before party:

• Bake Caramelized Vidalia Onion Dip.

• Grill Flat Iron Steak, and assemble crostini.

• Bake Mini Sun-dried Tomato Cheese Toasts.

• Arrange Marinated Vegetables on serving platter.

• Pour Blood Orange Martinis into pitchers or martini glasses.

---

editor's favorite

Açaí-Berry Mulled Cider

The açaí-raspberry juice blend in this soothing brew features açai juice, a now readily available superfood packed with powerful antioxidants.

Prep: 7 min.   Cook: 1 hr., 2 min.

2	(1.5-liter) bottles apple cider
6	cups açaí-raspberry juice blend (we tested with Tropicana)
⅓	cup firmly packed light brown sugar
3	(3") cinnamon sticks
5	whole allspice
5	whole cloves
1	(1") piece fresh ginger, peeled
3	orange slices
3	lemon slices

Combine first 3 ingredients in a very large Dutch oven. Cook over medium-high heat, stirring until sugar dissolves.

Tie cinnamon sticks and next 3 ingredients in a cheesecloth bag; add spice bag to cider. Add orange and lemon slices. Bring mixture to a boil; reduce heat to medium-low, and simmer 45 minutes. Discard spice bag. **Yield: 18½ cups.**

editor's favorite • make ahead

Blood Orange Martinis

Serve this stunning sipper in miniature, sugar-rimmed martini glasses.

Prep: 6 min.

4	cups blood orange juice
2	cups orange-flavored vodka
1	cup orange liqueur
	Simple Syrup
	Garnish: blood orange slices
	Coarse sugar (optional)

Combine first 4 ingredients in a large pitcher. Cover and chill until ready to serve. Garnish, if desired. Serve in sugar-rimmed glasses, if desired. **Yield: about 8 cups.**

Note: For sugared rims, dip rims of stemmed glasses into a thin coating of light corn syrup or water, and then spin rims in a plateful of coarse sugar.

Simple Syrup:

Prep: 1 min.   Cook: 6 min.   Other: 1 hr.

½   cup sugar

Bring sugar and ½ cup water to a boil in a saucepan. Boil, stirring often, 3 minutes or until sugar dissolves and syrup is reduced to ⅔ cup. Remove from heat; cool completely. Store in refrigerator. **Yield: ⅔ cup.**

gift idea • make ahead

Mediterranean Roasted Almonds

A gourmet sea salt blend is the star ingredient that transforms plain almonds into a memorable snack.

Prep: 9 min.   Cook: 45 min.

2   egg whites
2   tsp. Worcestershire sauce
2   (10-oz.) packages whole natural almonds
3   Tbsp. Mediterranean spiced sea salt
     (we tested with McCormick)
3   Tbsp. sugar
1   tsp. garlic powder
¼   tsp. dried crushed red pepper

Preheat oven to 300°. Whisk together egg whites, Worcestershire sauce, and 1 Tbsp. water in a large bowl until frothy. Add nuts, stirring to coat.

Combine sea salt and next 3 ingredients in another bowl. Using a slotted spoon, transfer coated nuts to spice mixture; toss well to coat nuts. Transfer nuts with a slotted spoon to a lightly greased large rimmed baking sheet, spreading nuts into a single layer.

Bake at 300° for 45 minutes, stirring after 25 minutes. Remove almonds from oven; cool completely on wire racks to help nuts dry out and gain some crunch. Store in airtight containers up to 1 month. **Yield: 5 cups.**

Blood Orange Martinis

Caramelized Vidalia Onion Dip

Here's a new take on an old favorite appetizer. Look for sturdy sweet potato chips for scooping up this mega-cheesy family favorite.

Prep: 14 min.   Cook: 1 hr., 10 min.

2	Tbsp. butter
3	large Vidalia or other sweet onions, thinly sliced
1	(8-oz.) package cream cheese, softened
1	(8-oz.) block Swiss cheese, shredded
1	cup freshly grated Parmesan cheese
1	cup regular or light mayonnaise

Sweet potato chips

Preheat oven to 375°. Melt butter in a large skillet over medium heat; add sliced onions. Cook, stirring often, 30 to 40 minutes or until onions are caramel colored.

Combine onions, cream cheese, and next 3 ingredients, stirring well. Spoon dip into a lightly greased 1½- to 2-qt. baking dish. Bake, uncovered, at 375° for 30 minutes or until golden and bubbly. Serve with sweet potato chips. **Yield: 4 cups.**

Make Ahead: Prepare dip a day ahead, but do not bake. Cover and refrigerate overnight. Bake, uncovered, at 375° for 45 minutes or until golden and bubbly.

Fig, Prosciutto, and Blue Cheese Squares

Refrigerated pizza crust dough unrolls to almost the perfect dimensions needed for this recipe. Briefly heating the oil and garlic infuses the oil with garlic flavor before it is brushed on the dough. This is a uniquely flavored appetizer pizza not to be missed.

Prep: 14 min.   Cook: 26 min.   Other: 5 min.

2	Tbsp. olive oil
2	garlic cloves, pressed
3	oz. thinly sliced prosciutto, chopped
1	(11-oz.) can refrigerated thin pizza crust dough
1	Tbsp. chopped fresh rosemary
½	cup fig preserves (we tested with Braswell's)
¾	cup crumbled blue cheese
½	tsp. freshly ground pepper

Garnishes: fresh rosemary, figs

Preheat oven to 400°. Combine oil and garlic in a small microwave-safe bowl. Microwave at HIGH 20 seconds or just until warm. Let stand while prosciutto cooks.

Cook prosciutto in a large skillet over medium-high heat 11 minutes or until browned and crisp; remove prosciutto, and drain on paper towels.

Unroll dough, and place on a lightly greased large baking sheet. Press out dough with hands to form a 15" x 13" rectangle. Brush dough with garlic-flavored oil; sprinkle rosemary over dough. Spread fig preserves over dough; sprinkle with prosciutto, cheese, and pepper.

Bake at 400° for 15 minutes or until crust is browned and crisp. Let stand 5 minutes before cutting. **Yield: 3 dozen.**

Make Ahead: Cook prosciutto up to 2 days ahead. Store in an airtight container in refrigerator until ready to assemble recipe.

Caramelized Vidalia Onion Dip

Fig, Prosciutto,
and Blue Cheese Squares

Marinated Vegetables (recipe on
following page)

Marinated Vegetables

Hosts will welcome this colorful make-ahead vegetable dish for the party table. Whole green beans or asparagus spears can be substituted for broccoli. (shown on page 15)

Prep: 17 min.   Cook: 3 min.   Other: 8 hr.

1   (12-oz.) package fresh broccoli florets
4   medium carrots, cut into thin (2") sticks
1   yellow, orange, or red bell pepper, cut into
     thin strips
1   lb. fresh button or baby portobello mushrooms
1   (5.75-oz.) jar pimiento-stuffed Spanish olives,
     drained
1   cup pitted kalamata olives, drained
¾   cup Italian white wine vinegar
2   Tbsp. sugar
1   tsp. salt
½   tsp. freshly ground black pepper
½   tsp. dried oregano
½   cup olive oil
1   (12-oz.) jar roasted red bell peppers, drained
     and cut into ½"-thick strips

Combine first 6 ingredients in a large bowl.
   Combine vinegar and next 4 ingredients in a small saucepan; bring to a boil. Reduce heat, and cook 1 minute or until sugar dissolves. Remove from heat; whisk in oil. Pour over vegetables in bowl; toss gently to coat. Add roasted red bell pepper; toss gently.
   Transfer vegetables to a 2-gal. zip-top plastic freezer bag. Seal and chill 8 hours, turning bag occasionally.
   Drain vegetables, reserving marinade. Arrange vegetables on a serving platter; drizzle with a small amount of reserved marinade, if desired. **Yield: 15 to 18 appetizer servings.**

Mini Muffulettas

Make these small bites of New Orleans up to 2 days ahead. The longer the flavorful Olive Salad marinade soaks into the sandwiches, the tastier they'll be.

Prep: 37 min.

28   (1.1-oz.) crusty bakery rolls, split (see note)
Olive Salad
28   thin slices Genoa salami (about ¾ lb.)
¾   lb. very thinly sliced deli ham
28   (.76-oz.) slices provolone cheese
Garnish: pimiento-stuffed olives

Arrange bottom halves of rolls on work surface. For each sandwich, spoon about 1 Tbsp. Olive Salad on a roll bottom. Layer salami, ham, and cheese over salad. Spoon 1 Tbsp. more Olive Salad over cheese, and cover with top of roll. Cut in half, and secure with wooden picks. Garnish, if desired. Store in an airtight container in refrigerator up to 2 days before serving. **Yield: 28 sandwiches.**

Note: Muffulettas are traditionally made with a crusty, round French loaf. For our minis, look for small crusty rolls that are about 1 oz. each and 2" to 4" in diameter. We tested with "water rolls."

Olive Salad:

Prep: 15 min.

1   (12-oz.) jar roasted red bell peppers with garlic
     and oregano, undrained (we tested with B&G)
1   (13-oz.) jar pimiento-stuffed Spanish olives, drained
1   (6-oz.) can pitted ripe black olives, drained
½   cup coarsely chopped red onion
5   pepperoncini peppers, cut in half
3   garlic cloves, cut in half
2   tsp. dried Italian seasoning
¼   cup olive oil
¼   tsp. freshly ground black pepper

Drain roasted red bell peppers; reserve 1 Tbsp. liquid.
   Pulse all ingredients and reserved liquid in a food processor until coarsely chopped. Cover and store in refrigerator until ready to use. **Yield: 4¾ cups.**

Mini Muffulettas

Grilled Flat-Iron Steak Crostini

Grilled Flat-Iron Steak Crostini

Store-bought crostini are slathered with herbed caper butter and topped with steak to make these elegant bites that are impressive but easy.

Prep: 10 min.   Cook: 10 min.   Other: 8 hr., 10 min.

1   Tbsp. chopped fresh rosemary
4   garlic cloves, minced
2   Tbsp. olive oil
1   Tbsp. lemon juice
2   lb. flat iron steak
¾   tsp. kosher salt
½   tsp. freshly ground pepper
Herbed Caper Butter
1   (7-oz.) container crostini
Garnish: fresh rosemary

Combine first 4 ingredients in a small bowl; rub over steak. Cover and chill 8 hours.

Preheat grill. Sprinkle steak with salt and pepper. Grill steak, covered with grill lid, over medium-high heat (350° to 400°) for 5 minutes on each side or until desired degree of doneness. Let stand 10 minutes. Cut diagonally across the grain into thin strips.

Spread Herbed Caper Butter over crostini; top with steak slices. Garnish, if desired. **Yield: 46 crostini.**

Herbed Caper Butter:

Prep: 6 min.

1   cup butter, softened
1   Tbsp. drained, chopped capers
1   Tbsp. chopped fresh parsley
1½   tsp. chopped fresh rosemary
½   tsp. lemon zest

Stir together all ingredients in a small bowl. **Yield: about 1¼ cups.**

Make Ahead: Prepare Herbed Caper Butter a day ahead; cover and refrigerate overnight. Let butter soften before spreading onto crostini.

Mini Sun-dried Tomato Cheese Toasts

Think gourmet grilled cheese with a surprise bite of sun-dried tomato hidden inside. These appetizers travel straight from the freezer to the oven. The large yield makes enough to serve for a party, to give as gifts to friends, and still have a few left to enjoy with a glass of wine on a cold January night.

Prep: 1 hr., 13 min.   Cook: 18 min. per batch
Other: 2 hr., 45 min.

2   (5-oz.) jars sharp process cheese spread
     (we tested with Old English)
¾   cup butter, softened
½   cup crumbled feta cheese
¾   tsp. dried basil
½   tsp. garlic powder
¼   tsp. ground red pepper
2   (16-oz.) loaves sandwich bread, chilled
     (we tested with Pepperidge Farm)
1   (10-oz.) jar sun-dried tomato pesto sauce
     (we tested with Classico)

Beat first 3 ingredients at medium speed with an electric mixer until creamy; stir in basil, garlic powder, and red pepper.

Work with 1 bread loaf at a time, leaving remainder chilled. Stack 4 slices of bread on a cutting board; remove crusts using a serrated knife. Spread 1 tsp. sun-dried tomato pesto over 1 slice bread; stack with another slice of bread. Spread cheese mixture over top and sides of sandwich; cut into 4 squares. Spread cheese mixture on bare sides of each square. Place stacks on an ungreased baking sheet; place in freezer 45 minutes or until firm. Repeat procedure with remaining bread loaf, pesto, and cheese mixture; freeze 45 minutes.

Transfer partially frozen squares from baking sheet to a large zip-top plastic freezer bag. Freeze 2 hours or up to 1 month.

Preheat oven to 350°. Place frozen squares on ungreased baking sheets. Bake at 350° for 18 minutes or until lightly browned and toasted. **Yield: 6 dozen.**

Note: A small amount of cheese may ooze onto the baking sheets during baking. We call this a good thing.

Dark Chocolate-Toffee Brownie Shooters

You'll get your chocolate fix in short order with these shot glasses of decadent mousse and brownie chunks doused with Kahlúa.

Prep: 47 min.   Cook: 30 min.   Other: 2 hr.

1   (18-oz.) package triple-chocolate brownie mix
      (we tested with Duncan Hines Triple Chocolate
      Decadence)
3   Tbsp. Kahlúa (optional)
3   (3.5-oz.) dark chocolate with toffee bits and
      caramelized almonds candy bars, chopped
      (we tested with Ghirardelli)
1½ cups whipping cream, divided
6   Tbsp. caramel topping
1   (7-oz.) can refrigerated instant nondairy whipped
      topping (we tested with Cool Whip)
Garnish: fresh mint sprigs

Bake brownies according to package directions for fudgy brownies. If desired, poke holes in baked brownies using a straw, and pour Kahlúa over brownies, allowing it to seep into holes. Let cool completely in pan.

Microwave chocolate and ¼ cup whipping cream in a large microwave-safe bowl at HIGH 1 to 1½ minutes or until chocolate melts, stirring after 1 minute. Let stand 45 minutes or until almost cool.

Beat remaining 1¼ cups whipping cream at high speed with an electric mixer until soft peaks form; gently fold into chocolate mixture.

Crumble brownies into bite-size pieces. Layer brownies, caramel topping, and chocolate mousse into 2-oz. shot glasses. Top each dessert shot with whipped topping. Garnish, if desired. **Yield: 3 dozen.**

Fix It Faster: Substitute 2 (8.6-oz.) packages Soft Baked Chocolate Chunk Brownie Cookies (we tested with Pepperidge Farm) for brownies. Toss crumbled cookies with Kahlúa, if desired.

Make Ahead: Make brownies up to 2 days before assembly. Assemble shooters up to 4 hours before party; cover and chill until ready to serve. Don't prepare mousse until ready to assemble desserts; it firms up quickly.

Dark Chocolate-Toffee Brownie
Shooters

SIX STANDOUT *Sideboards*

Holiday dining tables are laden with bowls and platters, plates and glasses—there's barely room for an extra fork, much less a centerpiece. What to do? Look to the sideboard as a perfect place to set the mood with a little seasonal splendor.

Rustic Yet Refined

Let an intriguing container, such as this faux bois planter, inspire the theme of your sideboard setting. Choose items that reinforce the idea, and use them in unexpected ways. Here, barklike pillar candles go in the planter, and pots of paperwhites light up the lanterns. Add easy embellishments, such as sheet moss, tufts of chartreuse reindeer moss, and moss-covered craft foam balls, to link the separate pieces for a pulled-together look. Insert sprigs of bright red berries to fill in and add a cheery note of color. The best thing about this arrangement? It will last all season long. If the paperwhite blooms fade, replace them with fresh pots of blooms or with pots of small evergreen trees, such as cedar and cypress.

Here's How

To make a citrus garland, thread tangerines onto a thin wire. Embellish ends with ribbons and seeded eucalyptus, greenery, or berries.

Rise & Dine

Begin the holiday celebration early with a sideboard setup that's perfect for a light breakfast. Consider white plates and serving pieces for a crisp contrast to dark wood surfaces. Accent with bright berries and fruits. To save space on a small sideboard, serve food on tiered servers or stacked cake stands. Nestle carafes of juice in a large metal container filled with crushed ice. Place flatware in a big bowl or mug, and pile napkins high on top of a plate. Greet guests with a message written on a whimsical chalkboard, such as this rooster.

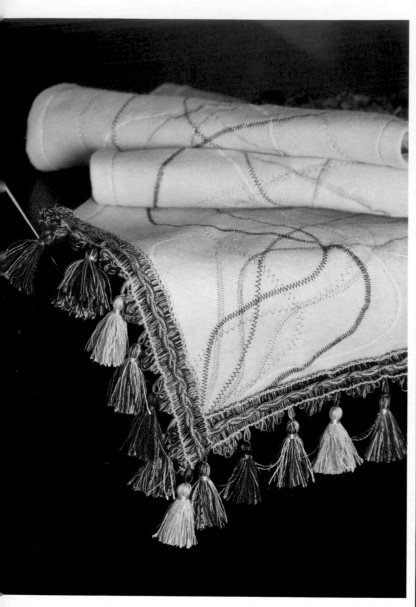

Quick-and-Easy Felt Table Runners

Felt is fabulous for do-it-yourself decorations. To make a quick runner for your sideboard or dining table, cut a length of felt to the desired size. Decorate the felt with your choice of fabric cutouts, sequins, and trims. For the design shown in the photo above, use a zigzag stitch to make a random pattern the length of the runner. Trim the short ends into a point, stitch under the long side edges, and finish by sewing a tasseled trim along each end. Directions for the red, no-sew runner are on the opposite page.

Felt is a perfect material for making all sorts of holiday decorations. It's easy to work with and inexpensive, and since it doesn't ravel, there's no need to finish raw edges.

Here's How
For the red table runner, cut designs from fabric and attach to the felt using fusible web (we used Wonder Under). Use fabric glue to attach sequins.

Snow Beautiful
As quick as you can say "let it snow" you'll have this sideboard arrangement set up and ready for a party. A glittery cardboard snow village is the backdrop for a dreamy hot chocolate bar. Arrange ivory pillar candles and white plates and mugs on the tabletop. Scatter fake snow around the candles and throw in a few red ornaments and striped candy canes for a punch of cheery color. Fill clear containers with cocoa mix, fluffy marshmallows, and toppings.

Bright Attitude

Assemble this super-simple setup in under 10 minutes. Top the sideboard with a table runner or length of fabric. Place cake stands topped with pillar candles on the runner. Sprinkle fake snowflakes around the cake stands and candles. Fill in with small ornaments and sprigs of silvery foliage. Finished!

Even everyday dinnerware gets in the holiday spirit when artfully arranged against a bright red wall and punctuated with Christmassy berries.

ELF *Party*

Join the elf craze by hosting this fanciful party for little ones. Elf cookies, milkshakes, party bags, a whimsical centerpiece, and more will magically appear when you follow our easy game plan.

menu
✥

Fruit Skewers With Strawberry Dip

Turkey Roll-Ups

Honey-Glazed Munchie Mix

Crispy Cookie Wands

Elf Cookies

Oatmeal Turtle Bars

Peppermint Milkshakes

serves 10 to 12

For a colorful centerpiece, fill glass jars with holiday candies. Let little guests scoop candies into paper takeout boxes for party favors.

Fruit Skewers With Strawberry Dip

Colorful, kid-friendly fruit on sticks gives the little ones an opportunity for dipping during the party. Any flavor yogurt works fine as the dip.

Prep: 20 min.

¼   cup pineapple juice
1   medium Braeburn apple, cut into small chunks
1   medium Granny Smith apple, cut into small chunks
12   seedless red grapes
12   seedless green grapes
12   large fresh strawberries, halved
12   (6") wooden skewers*
2   (6-oz.) containers strawberry cheesecake yogurt (we tested with Yoplait)

Combine pineapple juice and 2 Tbsp. water in a large bowl. Add apple chunks to bowl, tossing with juice to coat fruit.

Thread 1 piece of each color apple, 1 of each grape, and 2 strawberry halves onto each skewer. Serve fruit skewers with yogurt for dipping. **Yield: 12 servings.**

Make Ahead: Make skewers up to 3 hours before party. The pineapple juice keeps apples from turning brown.

* Plastic coffee stirrers can be substituted for wooden skewers if the points of skewers are a concern for young children.

Fruit Skewers With
Strawberry Dip,
Turkey Roll-Ups

make ahead
Turkey Roll-Ups

This recipe offers 3 different cheeses rolled up in deli-smoked turkey so there are options to suit everybody.

Prep: 11 min.

8   thin slices deli white American cheese
26 slices (about 1 lb.) thinly sliced deli smoked turkey (we tested with Sara Lee)
8   thin slices deli orange American cheese
1   (8-oz.) container cream cheese, softened

Place 1 slice white American cheese on 1 turkey slice; roll up tightly, and place, seam side down, on a cutting board. Repeat procedure with 7 more turkey slices and remaining white American cheese. Repeat procedure with 8 more slices turkey slices and orange American cheese slices; place roll-ups, seam side down, on cutting board.

Spread about 1 Tbsp. cream cheese onto each of remaining 10 turkey slices; roll up. (Reserve remaining cream cheese for another use.) Cut roll-ups in half diagonally, if desired. Arrange roll-ups on a serving platter. Cover and chill up to 24 hours. **Yield: 26 roll-ups.**

editor's favorite • make ahead
Honey-Glazed Munchie Mix

This snack has just the right mix of ingredients to keep kids of all ages coming back for seconds.

Prep: 10 min. Cook: 35 min. Other: 10 min.

3 cups sweet and salty honey-nut snack mix (we tested with Chex Mix)
3 cups dark chocolate snack mix (we tested with Chocolate Chex Mix)
2 cups fish-shaped pretzel crackers (we tested with Goldfish)
2 cups honey-flavored bear-shaped graham crackers (we tested with Teddy Grahams)
¼ cup butter
¼ cup light corn syrup
2 Tbsp. honey
1 tsp. vanilla extract
Wax paper
1 (13-oz.) package bear-shaped chewy candy (we tested with Gummy Bears)
1 (14-oz.) package candy-coated chocolate pieces

Preheat oven to 325°. Combine first 4 ingredients in a large bowl.

Heat butter and next 3 ingredients in a small saucepan over medium-low heat, stirring until butter melts. Pour over snack mixture, stirring until well coated. Spread snack mix on a 15½" x 10½" jelly-roll pan.

Bake at 325° for 30 minutes, stirring every 10 minutes. Spread snack mix on wax paper; let cool 10 minutes. Add candy bears and chocolate pieces; toss well with fingers. Store in a large zip-top plastic freezer bag up to 1 week. **Yield: 14 cups.**

Honey-Glazed Munchie Mix

Crispy Cookie Wands

These cookie wands taste like a familiar rice cereal treat, but we've put them on sticks all decorated for little holiday elves.

Prep: 16 min.   Cook: 25 min.

3   Tbsp. butter
1   (10-oz.) package large marshmallows
6   cups crisp rice cereal (we tested with Rice Krispies)
Wax paper
16   round white or holiday-colored craft sticks
4   oz. white chocolate, coarsely chopped
2   Tbsp. whipping cream
Colored sprinkles

Melt butter in a Dutch oven over medium-low heat. Add marshmallows; stir until completely melted. Remove from heat; add cereal, stirring until coated.

Using a lightly greased spoon, firmly pack cereal mixture into a lightly greased 13" x 9" pan. Cool completely in pan.

Cut cereal treats into 16 rectangles. Place rectangles on wax paper. Carefully push a craft stick into 1 short end of each rectangle.

Combine white chocolate and cream in top of a double boiler over hot, not simmering, water. Cook, stirring often,
until smooth. Spoon white chocolate mixture into a 1-qt. zip-top plastic freezer bag. (Do not seal.) Snip 1 corner of bag with scissors to make a small hole. Pipe white chocolate over rectangles; decorate with sprinkles. **Yield: 16 cookie wands.**

Make Ahead: Prepare cookie wands up to 1 day ahead. Place on a tray between layers of wax paper. Cover tightly with aluminum foil, and store in refrigerator.

Note: Find craft sticks (the kind used to make lollipops) in the candy-making section of a hobby store.

Elf Cookies

Start with store-bought cookie dough and an elf-themed cookie cutter and let cookie decorating be the kids' project during party time.

Prep: 18 min.   Cook: 12 min. per batch   Other: 15 min.

2   (19-oz.) packages sugar cookie dough sheets
     (we tested with Pillsbury)
Parchment paper
1   egg white, lightly beaten
Red and green coarse decorator sugars
1   (6.4-oz.) can white decorating icing (we tested
     with Betty Crocker)
48   milk chocolate or semisweet chocolate morsels

Preheat oven to 350°. Using an elf face-shaped cookie cutter, cut out dough (we used a 5" x 4" copper elf face cutter from www.thecookiecuttershop.com). Reroll trimmings to make additional cookies.

Place cutouts 1" apart on parchment paper-lined large baking sheets. Brush hats and bowties of elves with egg white; sprinkle with decorator sugars.

Bake at 350° for 10 to 12 minutes or until edges are lightly browned. Cool 5 minutes on baking sheets; remove to wire racks to cool completely.

Squirt 2 drops of icing onto each cookie face for eyes. Top each drop of icing with a chocolate morsel. **Yield: 2 dozen.**

Note: Find sugar cookie dough sheets in the dairy case of your grocery store during the holiday season.

Elf Cookies

Crispy Cookie
Wands

Oatmeal Turtle Bars

Here's a deluxe bar cookie for moms to nibble on while the kids enjoy some elf mischief.

Prep: 29 min.   Cook: 62 min.   Other: 8 hr.

Heavy-duty aluminum foil
1   (14-oz.) package caramels
1   (14-oz.) can sweetened condensed milk
1½   cups unsalted butter, softened
1½   cups granulated sugar
1½   cups firmly packed brown sugar
2   large eggs, lightly beaten
1   tsp. vanilla extract
3   cups all-purpose flour
1   tsp. baking powder
1   tsp. salt
½   tsp. baking soda
2½   cups uncooked quick-cooking oats
1   (12-oz.) package semisweet chocolate morsels
1   (6-oz.) package semisweet chocolate morsels
1   cup chopped pecans

Line a greased 13" x 9" pan with heavy-duty aluminum foil, allowing several inches of foil to extend over sides. Lightly grease foil.

Combine caramels and milk in a medium saucepan. Cook over low heat, stirring often, 22 minutes or until caramels melt and mixture is smooth. Set aside.

Preheat oven to 350°. Beat butter at medium speed with an electric mixer until creamy. Gradually add sugars, beating until smooth. Add eggs and vanilla, beating until blended.

Combine flour, baking powder, salt, and soda; gradually add to butter mixture, beating just until blended. Stir in oats.

Press 4 cups dough into prepared pan. Top with chocolate morsels and pecans. Pour caramel mixture over pecans. Crumble remaining dough over caramel.

Bake at 350° for 38 to 40 minutes or until golden. Cool completely in pan on a wire rack. Cover and chill 8 hours. Cut into small bars. Store in refrigerator up to 5 days.
Yield: 40 bars.

Peppermint Milkshakes

This yummy dessert drink appeals to all ages. Use less milk for really thick shakes.

Prep: 16 min.

8   cups vanilla ice cream
2   cups milk
1   cup crushed hard peppermint round candies
      (about 45 to 50 candies)
1   (8.5-oz.) can refrigerated instant whipped cream
      (we tested with Reddi-wip)
Peppermint sticks

Process 4 cups ice cream, 1 cup milk, and ½ cup crushed candies in a blender until smooth, stopping to scrape down sides as needed. Pour into small serving glasses; top with whipped cream, and place a peppermint stick in each glass. Repeat with remaining ingredients.
Yield: 9¼ cups.

Note: Process peppermint candies in a food processor for quick crushing.

Peppermint Milkshakes

COZY *Christmas Eve Dinner*

Set an intimate table for two and toast the season with this Mediterranean-inspired meal at fireside.

menu

Creamy Turnip Soup With Bacon, Caramelized
Pears, and Onions

Roast Pork With Provençal Breadcrumb Crust
and Sherry Glaze

Greens With Goat Cheese, Pecans, and Sherry
Vinaigrette

Broccoli With Roasted Garlic and Tomatoes

Mini Chocolate-Cherry Layer Cakes

serves 2

1 day ahead:

• Prepare chocolate-cherry cakes; chill.

• Prepare turnip soup (but not the bacon, pear, and onion topping); chill.

• Prepare and chill Sherry Glaze.

• Prepare and chill salad dressing.

• Roast and chill garlic for broccoli.

2 hours before meal:

• Prepare breadcrumb crust, and roast the pork.

30 minutes before meal:

• Reheat soup; keep warm.

• While pork roasts, prepare bacon, caramelized pear, and onion topping for soup.

• While pork stands, roast broccoli and prepare salad.

• Plate the meal; pour wine and light a fire.

editor's favorite • make ahead

Creamy Turnip Soup With Bacon, Caramelized Pears, and Onions

Right before serving, prepare the bacon, pear, and onion topping.

Prep: 11 min. Cook: 44 min.

2   Tbsp. butter, divided
1   cup thinly sliced leek (about 1 small)
½   lb. turnips, peeled and diced ½" (1½ cups)
1   cup low-sodium fat-free chicken broth
3   Tbsp. whipping cream
¼   tsp. salt
¼   tsp. ground white pepper
1   bacon slice
½   firm pear, peeled and thinly sliced
½   small onion, halved and thinly sliced
2   tsp. sugar

Melt 1 Tbsp. butter in a medium-size heavy saucepan over medium heat. Add leeks; sauté 5 minutes or until

tender. Add turnips, chicken broth, and ½ cup water; bring to a boil. Cover, reduce heat, and simmer 20 minutes or until turnips are very tender.

Process soup, in batches, in a blender or food processor until smooth, stopping to scrape down sides as needed. Return to saucepan; stir in cream, salt, and pepper. Set aside, and keep warm.

Cook bacon in a large skillet over medium heat 5 minutes or until crisp; remove bacon, and drain on paper towels. Crumble bacon; set aside. Wipe skillet clean with a paper towel. Melt remaining 1 Tbsp. butter in skillet over medium-high heat. Add pear and onion; sprinkle with sugar. Sauté 9 to 11 minutes or until golden brown.

To serve, ladle soup into bowls, and top with crumbled bacon and pear mixture. **Yield: about 2 cups.**

editor's favorite

Roast Pork With Provençal Breadcrumb Crust

A French-inspired crusting gives this roast an incredible aroma in the oven. Ask your butcher to french the roast for you. If you do it yourself, be sure to cut all the fat from the rib bones and scrape them clean to make a beautiful presentation.

Prep: 6 min.   Cook: 55 min.   Other: 15 min.

⅓   cup fresh breadcrumbs
¼   cup freshly grated Parmesan cheese
3   Tbsp. finely chopped pitted kalamata olives
1½   Tbsp. finely chopped fresh thyme
2   garlic cloves, pressed
3   Tbsp. olive oil, divided
1   (3-rib) (1¼- to 1½-lb.) pork loin roast, frenched
Salt and freshly ground pepper
3   Tbsp. Sherry Glaze

Preheat oven to 350°. Combine first 5 ingredients in a small bowl; stir in 2 Tbsp. oil.

Place pork roast, bone side down, in a small greased roasting pan. Rub remaining 1 Tbsp. oil over meaty top side of roast; sprinkle with desired amount of salt and pepper, and pat breadcrumb mixture over oil to adhere.

Bake at 350° for 45 to 55 minutes or until a thermometer inserted into thickest portion registers 155°. Let stand 15 minutes or until thermometer registers 160°. Carve roast between bones into 3 chops. Drizzle each serving with Sherry Glaze. **Yield: 2 to 3 servings.**

Sherry Glaze:

Reserve 1 tablespoon of this glaze for the next recipe.

Prep: 1 min.   Cook: 18 min.

2   cups cream sherry

Bring sherry to a boil in a medium saucepan over medium-high heat; boil until syrupy and reduced to ¼ cup. Remove from heat; let cool. **Yield: ¼ cup.**

Note: To make a non-alcoholic reduction, substitute 1 cup apple cider for cream sherry. Bring cider to a boil over medium-high heat in a small saucepan; boil 15 minutes or until reduced to ¼ cup.

quick & easy
Greens With Goat Cheese, Pecans, and Sherry Vinaigrette

Prep: 4 min.

1   Tbsp. Sherry Glaze (see recipe above)
1½   tsp. sherry vinegar
¼   tsp. salt
¼   tsp. freshly ground pepper
1½   Tbsp. extra virgin olive oil
3   cups mixed baby greens
1   oz. goat cheese, crumbled
¼   cup sugared pecans (we tested with Hoody's)*

Combine first 4 ingredients in a small bowl, stirring with a wire whisk; gradually whisk in oil.

Place greens on 2 salad plates. Sprinkle salads with goat cheese and pecans; drizzle with vinaigrette. **Yield: 2 servings.**

*Substitute Praline Pecans (page 161) for the store-bought sugared pecans, if desired.

Broccoli With Roasted Garlic and Tomatoes

Roasted broccoli and tomatoes make a festive pairing for pork.

Prep: 5 min.   Cook: 42 min.
Heavy-duty aluminum foil
4   large garlic cloves
3   cups broccoli florets (7 oz.)
1   Tbsp. olive oil
1   cup grape tomatoes
2   Tbsp. unsalted butter, softened
¼   tsp. salt
¼   tsp. freshly ground pepper
3   Tbsp. freshly grated Parmesan cheese (optional)

Preheat oven to 425°. Fold a sheet of foil in half, creasing it to form a double sheet. Place garlic in center; drizzle with 1 tsp. water. Fold foil to seal. Bake at 425° for 20 minutes or until lightly browned and tender. Transfer to a small bowl; mash garlic with a fork. Increase oven temperature to 450°.

Combine garlic, broccoli, and oil in a lightly greased cast-iron skillet. Spread vegetables in a single layer.

Roast at 450° for 10 minutes or until broccoli begins to brown. Add tomatoes and next 3 ingredients to skillet, tossing to combine. Roast 12 more minutes or until tomato skins begin to split. Sprinkle with cheese, if desired. **Yield: 2 servings.**

Mini Chocolate-Cherry
Layer Cakes

Mini Chocolate-Cherry Layer Cakes

Share one of these tender-rich chocolate mousse cakes with your sweetie, and freeze the other up to 2 weeks.

Prep: 13 min.   Cook: 20 min.   Other: 2 hr., 55 min.

Parchment paper
¼   cup all-purpose flour
¼   cup unsweetened cocoa
¼   tsp. salt
3   large eggs, at room temperature
½   cup sugar
2   tsp. hot water
2   Tbsp. unsalted butter, melted
Cherry Syrup
Chocolate Mousse
Chocolate Glaze
Garnish: cherries with stems

Preheat oven to 400°. Grease an 8" square cake pan. Line bottom of pan with parchment paper; flour edges of pan. Set aside.

Sift ¼ cup flour, cocoa, and salt into a small bowl. Combine eggs, sugar, and hot water in a small, deep bowl; beat at medium-high speed with an electric mixer 5 minutes or until thick and pale. Sift half of flour mixture over egg mixture; gently fold into egg mixture. Repeat procedure with remaining flour mixture. Drizzle butter over batter; fold butter into batter. (Do not overmix.) Pour batter into prepared pan.

Bake at 400° for 17 to 20 minutes or until a wooden pick inserted in center comes out clean. Cool in pan on a wire rack 10 minutes; remove from pan to a wire rack to cool completely.

Brush Cherry Syrup over cake. Cut cake into 4 squares. Spoon Chocolate Mousse onto 2 cake squares, spreading to edges. Place remaining 2 squares on top of mousse, and press gently to adhere. Chill 30 minutes.

Pour Chocolate Glaze over cakes, spreading to cover tops and sides. Chill 2 to 24 hours before serving. Garnish, if desired. **Yield: 4 servings.**

Cherry Syrup:

Prep: 4 min.

3   Tbsp. cherry preserves
2   tsp. cherry brandy or ¼ tsp. almond extract

Press preserves through a fine wire-mesh strainer into a bowl using the back of a spoon to yield 2 Tbsp. sieved preserves; stir in liqueur. **Yield: about 3 Tbsp.**

Chocolate Mousse:

Prep: 3 min.   Cook: 1 min.

1½   oz. bittersweet chocolate, finely chopped (about ⅓ cup)
⅓   cup whipping cream

Microwave chocolate in a small microwave-safe bowl at HIGH 30 seconds or until chocolate melts; stir until smooth. While chocolate is warm, beat whipping cream with an electric mixer until stiff peaks form; beat in chocolate. **Yield: ¾ cup.**

Chocolate Glaze:

Prep: 1 min.   Cook: 3 min.   Other: 15 min.

⅓   cup whipping cream
1   Tbsp. light corn syrup
2   oz. bittersweet chocolate, finely chopped (about ½ cup)
2   tsp. cherry brandy or ¼ tsp. almond extract

Bring whipping cream and corn syrup to a boil in a small saucepan. Remove from heat; stir in chocolate and liqueur. Stir until smooth. Cool 15 minutes or until mixture is thickened but still pourable. **Yield: ½ cup.**

FAMILY *Celebration*

Host a crowd of loved ones with this bounteous meal that begins with a beautiful cocktail and ends with two luscious sweets. And the dinner plate will win raves in between.

menu

Prosecco Splash

Roasted Root Vegetable Bisque

Ham With Bourbon, Cola, and Cherry Glaze

Holiday Potato Bake

Roasted Brussels Sprouts and Cauliflower
With Bacon Dressing

Pear and Pecan Frangipane Galette

Chocolate-Orange Velvet Tart

serves 12

Serve sparkling Prosecco Splash in stemless champagne flutes on a metal tray. Cheers!

editor's favorite • quick & easy

Prosecco Splash

Dress up Prosecco, an Italian sparkling wine, with a splash of pomegranate liqueur and a few frozen berries for a festive cocktail.

Prep: 10 min.

3⅓ cups pomegranate liqueur (we tested with PAMA)
2   (750-milliliter) bottles Prosecco, chilled
Frozen blackberries and raspberries

Spoon 3 Tbsp. pomegranate liqueur into each of 18 champagne flutes. Pour Prosecco into each flute, filling two-thirds full. Drop a frozen blackberry and raspberry into each glass. Serve immediately. **Yield: 18 servings.**

make ahead

Roasted Root Vegetable Bisque

This appetizer soup will get your family gathering off to a delicious start. It's a thick puree of winter's best ingredients, blended with cream and Cajun seasoning.

Prep: 35 min.   Cook: 1 hr., 38 min.

6   parsnips, peeled and chopped (1 lb.)
4   small turnips, peeled and chopped (1 lb.)
2   medium celeriac, peeled and chopped (1 lb.)
1   large butternut squash, peeled and chopped (2 lb.)
¼   cup olive oil
10   cups chicken broth, divided
¼   cup butter
1   large onion, chopped (about 2 cups)
4   garlic cloves, minced
3   Tbsp. all-purpose flour
3   Tbsp. tomato paste
2   tsp. Cajun seasoning
1   cup heavy whipping cream
½   tsp. salt

Preheat oven to 450°. Combine parsnips and next 4 ingredients in a large bowl; toss to coat. Transfer vegetables into a large roasting pan, spreading into 1 layer.

Roast at 450° for 1 hour to 1 hour and 10 minutes or until very tender and browned. Process half of roasted vegetables and 3 cups chicken broth in a blender until smooth. Pour vegetable puree into a large pot. Repeat with remaining roasted vegetables and 3 cups chicken broth; set aside.

Melt butter in a large skillet over medium-high heat; add onion and garlic, and sauté 7 minutes. Reduce heat to medium. Add flour; cook, stirring constantly, 3 minutes or until browned. Stir in tomato paste and Cajun seasoning; cook, stirring often, 3 minutes. Process onion mixture and remaining 4 cups chicken broth in blender until smooth. Transfer to pot with vegetable mixture. Stir in cream and salt. Bring to a boil over medium heat; reduce heat to medium-low, and simmer, stirring often, 15 minutes. **Yield: 17 cups.**

Make Ahead: Prepare this soup up to the point of sautéing the onion. Freeze the pureed vegetable mixture in zip-top plastic freezer bags up to 1 month.

Ham With Bourbon, Cola, and Cherry Glaze

This holiday ham sizzles with Southern comfort. Pick a ham with a fat layer intact that will crisp up when baked and show off its pepper and clove crust.

Prep: 11 min.   Cook: 3 hr., 48 min.   Other: 1 hr.

1   (12- to 14-lb.) fully cooked, bone-in ham shank
1   Tbsp. black peppercorns
30   whole cloves
1   (12-oz.) can cola soft drink, divided
¼   cup bourbon, divided
6   Tbsp. firmly packed brown sugar, divided
1   (13-oz.) jar cherry preserves, divided (we tested with Bonne Maman)
Garnishes: kumquats, cherries

Preheat oven to 350°. Remove skin from ham; trim fat to ¼" thickness. Make shallow cuts in fat 1" apart in a diamond pattern. Place peppercorns in a small zip-top plastic freezer bag. Tap peppercorns with a meat mallet or small heavy skillet until coarsely crushed. Rub peppercorns over surface of ham; insert cloves in centers of diamonds. Insert a meat thermometer into ham, making sure it does not touch fat or bone. Place ham in a lightly greased 13" x 9" pan; set aside.

Combine ¼ cup cola, 2 Tbsp. bourbon, and 2 Tbsp. brown sugar; set aside. Combine remaining cola, bourbon, and brown sugar; pour over ham.

Bake at 350° for 2 hours, basting with cola mixture every 15 minutes. Remove ham from oven; leave oven on.

Ham With Bourbon, Cola, and Cherry Glaze

Meanwhile, combine reserved cola mixture and ⅔ cup cherry preserves in a medium saucepan. Cook over medium heat 3 minutes or until glaze is hot and sugar dissolves; brush ham with glaze. Return ham to oven; bake at 350° for 1 hour and 45 more minutes or until thermometer registers 140°. (Cover ham with aluminum foil during the last hour, if necessary, to prevent excessive browning.) Let ham stand 1 hour before carving.

Transfer baked ham to a serving platter; cover with foil. Remove fat from drippings in pan. Whisk remaining ½ cup cherry preserves into drippings in pan. Transfer mixture to a saucepan, if desired, or continue cooking in roasting pan placed over 2 burners on the stovetop. Bring to a boil; reduce heat, and simmer until slightly thickened (8 to 10 minutes). Serve glaze with ham. Garnish ham, if desired. **Yield: 12 to 14 servings.**

Holiday Potato Bake

Simple mashed potatoes get dressed up in this comfort food dish inspired by twice-baked potatoes.

Prep: 24 min.   Cook: 1 hr., 10 min.

6   large baking potatoes, peeled and cut into chunks
¼   cup butter
1   cup chopped green onions
4   garlic cloves, minced
2   cups milk
2   cups (8 oz.) shredded extra-sharp Cheddar cheese, divided
2   tsp. salt
1   (12-oz.) jar roasted red bell peppers, drained and finely chopped
4   oz. cream cheese, softened
2   large eggs, lightly beaten

Preheat oven to 375°. Cook potatoes in boiling water to cover 15 to 20 minutes or until tender; drain well.

Meanwhile, melt butter in a large skillet over medium-high heat; add green onions and garlic. Sauté 5 minutes or until tender.

Combine potatoes and green onion mixture in a large bowl; mash using a potato masher. Add milk, 1 cup cheese, and remaining ingredients; mash. Spoon into a lightly greased 13" x 9" baking dish. Top with remaining 1 cup cheese.

Bake at 375° for 45 to 50 minutes or until browned and bubbly. **Yield: 10 to 12 servings.**

Roasted Brussels Sprouts and Cauliflower
With Bacon Dressing

Roasted Brussels Sprouts and Cauliflower With Bacon Dressing

This is one of the best side dish offerings of the holiday season. Brussels sprouts and cauliflower develop a nutty flavor once roasted, and the bacon vinaigrette adds a smoky hit.

Prep: 29 min.   Cook: 48 min.

1½	lb. fresh Brussels sprouts
2	medium heads cauliflower (about 2 lb. each), cut into florets
¼	cup olive oil
2	Tbsp. sugar
10	bacon slices
2	Tbsp. white wine vinegar
1	Tbsp. olive oil
2	garlic cloves, minced
1	tsp. salt
½	tsp. pepper
¾	cup pitted kalamata olives, coarsely chopped
1	Tbsp. chopped fresh parsley
1	tsp. chopped fresh thyme

Preheat oven to 450°. Rinse Brussels sprouts thoroughly; remove any discolored leaves. Trim stem ends; cut in half lengthwise. Combine sprouts and next 3 ingredients in a large roasting pan; toss to coat. Spread into 1 layer. Roast at 450° for 45 to 48 minutes or until vegetables are tender and browned, stirring after 30 minutes.

Meanwhile, cook bacon in a large skillet over medium-high heat 15 minutes or until crisp; remove bacon, and drain on paper towels, reserving 2 Tbsp. drippings. Crumble bacon. Whisk together drippings, vinegar, and next 4 ingredients.

Drizzle vinaigrette over roasted vegetables. Add crumbled bacon, olives, parsley, and thyme; toss to coat. **Yield: 12 servings.**

Make Ahead: Cut vegetables up to 1 day ahead, and store them in airtight containers in refrigerator.

Pear and Pecan
Frangipane Galette

Chocolate-Orange
Velvet Tart

Pear and Pecan Frangipane Galette

Frangipane is a pastry filling made thick with ground almonds. This Southern version of a French-inspired dish couldn't be easier.

Prep: 1 hr.   Cook: 45 min.   Other: 20 min.

2¼   cups all-purpose flour
½   tsp. salt, divided
⅓   cup turbinado sugar
1   cup butter, softened and divided
3   egg yolks
1   cup pecan halves
½   cup granulated sugar
1   tsp. freshly ground cinnamon*
¼   tsp. freshly grated nutmeg*
6   firm Bartlett pears, peeled and sliced
    (about 2 lb.)
1   Tbsp. turbinado sugar
1   Tbsp. fresh lemon juice
Parchment paper
Garnish: unsweetened whipped cream

Whisk together flour, ¼ tsp. salt, and ⅓ cup turbinado sugar in a large bowl. Add ½ cup butter and egg yolks. Using your hands, gently combine mixture until it resembles small peas and dough is crumbly. Add 3 Tbsp. water until dough forms a smooth ball. (It's crucial to use your hands in this step, so you can feel the texture of the dough.) Flatten dough into a 1"-thick disk; wrap in plastic wrap, and chill 20 minutes.

While dough chills, process pecans, 6 Tbsp. butter, ½ cup granulated sugar, cinnamon, nutmeg, and remaining ¼ tsp. salt in a food processor 30 seconds. Scrape down sides; process 30 more seconds or until smooth. Set aside.

Preheat oven to 400°. Place remaining 2 Tbsp. butter in a large microwave-safe bowl. Microwave at HIGH 20 seconds or until melted. Add pear slices, 1 Tbsp. turbinado sugar, and lemon juice to butter, tossing until pears are coated.

Unwrap dough and place in center of a 16" x 15" piece of parchment paper. Cover dough with a 16" piece of plastic wrap. Roll out dough to a 16" circle. (Rolled dough will overhang edges of parchment ½" on each side.) Remove plastic wrap and carefully transfer parchment with dough onto a large baking sheet. Spread pecan filling over dough, leaving a 1" border around edges. Arrange pear mixture over filling to within 2" of edges. Fold a 2" border of dough over pears. Bake at 400° for 40 to 45 minutes or until well browned. Serve warm or at room temperature. Garnish, if desired. **Yield: 12 servings.**

*We tested with McCormick Cinnamon Grinder. Substitute ground cinnamon and nutmeg for the freshly ground and grated spices, if desired.

Chocolate-Orange Velvet Tart

This luxurious tart is more like a truffle than a pie. Serve slivers or slices; coffee's a must.

Prep: 27 min.   Cook: 15 min.   Other: 4 hr.

1¼   cups cinnamon-flavored graham cracker crumbs (about 8 sheets)
3   Tbsp. brown sugar
¼   cup butter, melted
¾   cup heavy whipping cream
½   cup milk
¼   cup turbinado sugar
1   Tbsp. orange zest
1   tsp. ground cinnamon
3   (4-oz.) semisweet chocolate baking bars, coarsely chopped (we tested with Ghirardelli)
Garnishes: sweetened whipped cream, orange zest

   Preheat oven to 375°. Combine first 3 ingredients; press firmly into a lightly greased 9" pie plate.
   Bake at 375° for 11 minutes or until lightly browned. Remove from oven; let cool.
   Combine cream and next 4 ingredients in a saucepan. Bring to a simmer over medium-low heat. Remove from heat; add chocolate, and stir until chocolate is melted and mixture is smooth. Pour filling into baked crust. Refrigerate 4 hours or until firm. Garnish, if desired.
Yield: 8 to 12 servings.

Impressive Table Touches
Here are three ideas for freshening up the holiday table.
• **Chandelier Cranberries.** For a beautiful addition to your table décor, fill bottoms of glass globes with fresh cranberries and add small candles (top right); suspend globes from your chandelier with sturdy ribbon. Light candles during the meal.
• **Button Napkin Rings.** Tuck a sprig of seeded eucalyptus or other Christmas greenery into a large-button napkin ring at each place setting (middle right).
• **Fancy Menu Display.** Use a dry erase pencil to write and display your holiday menu on a porcelain memo board (bottom right).

PARTY-READY *Tables*

If you can choose only one spot in your home to make the biggest holiday decorating impact, make it the dining table. Since it's the gathering spot for the most heartfelt celebrations, it deserves special treatment. These ideas will help you get started.

Topsy-turvy Tasting Party

A mix of wine glasses hanging upside-down from the chandelier tells guests that this is no stuffy wine-and-cheese party. Tie glasses to the overhead light fixture with varying lengths of ribbon. Knot the ribbon to be sure the glasses are held securely in place. To continue the theme, fill tall glass vases and wine glasses with fruits. To invert the vases, hold a flat plate on top of the vase

and flip it over. Carefully remove the plate from underneath the vase. To flip the wine glasses, placing your hand over the top of the glass should do the trick. Adorn the tops of the vases with single pieces of fruit or clusters of grapes. Use pottery plates and serving pieces for a casual ambience.

Ritzy Recycling

Transform an empty wine bottle into a chic table decoration. Place a metal wine bottle candelabra in the empty bottle, and voilá! It's a speedy table decoration that's both sophisticated and inexpensive. You'll find a vast array of candelabra styles online and in home specialty stores. Fit taper candles in the candelabra, or for extra pizzazz, use corklike candles (also found online). Enhance the centerpiece arrangement with small, wine split bottles filled with cranberries and sporting candles. Tie name tags on unopened splits, and set them in stemless wine glasses to serve as place markers. Fill the centermost bottle with arching twig clippings, sprigs of berries, and snippets of evergreens.

Assemble an eclectic mix of bottles for the most appealing display.

Simply Charming

Accessorize china, such as this blue-and-white transferware, with shiny accents to set a holiday table straight from your everyday china stash. Use silver pieces, like the mercury glass candleholders and pewter chargers, to convey a special-occasion air that's perfectly suited to any time of year.

Style Notes

Don't be intimidated by this fabulous center-piece—anyone can do it. Start by placing a pot of amaryllis in a container; wedge blocks of moistened floral foam around the pot, then stick in stems of flowers and greenery to cover the foam. Tie a ribbon around the amaryllis stems to hold them upright. Extend the floral flair to each place setting by using small vases as props for place cards. Mix in unexpected items, such as woven place mats, for a relaxed counterpoint to the dressier pieces on the table. Use snips of ribbon to add soft color to a neutral setting. At this table, the centerpiece, place cards, and napkins all benefit from a touch of blue velvet.

Merry Bells

Bring the glass bell jars in from the garden and use them for a fresh seasonal display. Select jars of all sizes for the most appealing effect. Place them over small pottery pieces and bowls holding tiny flower arrangements. Place blocks of moistened floral foam in the bowls to make flower arranging easy. Use red flowers and tuck bright green reindeer moss around the blooms for brilliant color.

Over the Top
Dangle flatware from
the chandelier for a
centerpiece that goes
above and beyond the
tabletop. Attach the
forks and spoons with
varying lengths of
sheer ribbon for a
staggered effect.

Fabric-fringed Table Topper

It only takes an afternoon to make this burlap table topper that puts fabric remnants from your sewing cabinet to excellent use. Cut a square of burlap to the desired size for your table. Use a pointed object, such as scissors, to punch holes at regular intervals along the edges of the burlap. Loop a long, unfinished strip of fabric through each hole.

Bright New Year

Use paper lanterns and fluttering butterflies to cast a spark of whimsy and start the new year in style. For this look, line the table with large and small lanterns, place branches of curly willow in the large lanterns, and wire paper butterflies to the branches. Pile richly colored ornaments in tall glass vases to give a nod to the holiday season, and fill takeout boxes with fortune cookies as take-home treats for guests.

Flameless candles are the ticket for illuminating paper lanterns. They're available in both votives and pillars.

Small Favors

Greet guests with a little something extra as they sit down to dine. Make good use of last year's cards to make glowing luminaries (opposite page). Trim cards, punch holes at the top and bottom edges, and tie together with ribbons. Place a votive holder and candle in the center.

For a fresh approach, cut two circles from heavy paper (above). Glue a floral pick between the circles. Wrap the pick with thin ribbon and finish with a bow. Stick the pick into a bright apple. Personalize with guests' names before gluing.

For a sweet surprise, fill paper cupcake liners with candies. Nestle a place card among the goodies (top right).

Delight guests with a Christmas cracker (bottom right). Trim a paper towel tube to the desired size. Fill the tube with tiny treats. Wrap the tube with cheery paper, tie the ends with ribbons, and use stickers for names.

EASY *Centerpieces*

*These out-of-the-ordinary table decorations are impressive yet simple to create.
Make the items in multiples and place them in a line down the table. After dinner,
let each guest select one of the individual arrangements as a take-home party favor.*

Have a Ball

Bright green moss balls perched in martini glasses add a fun update to a traditional setting. You can purchase moss balls online and at crafts stores, or you can make your own by gluing moss to craft foam spheres. To finish the table decoration, fill in with evergreen balls or use smaller versions of the moss balls. Provide candlelight by way of petite bouquets encircling taper candles. To make the bouquets, fill small containers with moistened floral foam. Anchor the candles in the foam and surround them with flower blooms and reindeer moss.

Can Do

With all the cooking and food preparation between Thanksgiving and New Year's Day, you're sure to have a good supply of empty food cans. Here's a nifty way to recycle those cans and transform them into cute centerpiece containers. Remove paper labels and wash the cans. Cut strips of heavy-stock paper, such as scrapbooking paper, into lengths to fit around each can. Fasten the paper in place using a glue gun or double-sided tape. Fill the cans with evergreen and berry clippings. Group several cans as a centerpiece. Scatter ornaments around the cans for a glittery touch.

Use leftover snippets of wrapping
paper to cover glass vases. Secure
paper edges with double-sided tape.
Tie bows around the vases, and fill
with a mix of candies, candles,
flowers, and greenery.

THE IDEAS ON THESE PAGES WILL INSPIRE YOU TO BRING THE SPARKLE AND JOY OF
THE SEASON TO EVERY ROOM IN YOUR HOUSE.

Decorating

WELCOMING *Style*

Greet friends and family with outdoor decorations that show your unique style.
The ideas on these pages suggest ways to express holiday cheer from the front door,
the garden, and even the mailbox.

Two for One

For a double-door entry, consider this idea for a two-piece wreath. Start with a regular wreath that has a sturdy base so it will hold its shape. A fresh evergreen wreath was used here, but a permanent wreath or grapevine wreath will work as well. Cut the wreath in half lengthwise. The type of wreath you have will determine what tool is needed to cut the wreath. Sturdy wire clippers should work in most cases. Use thin, flexible wire to attach evergreen clippings, fruits, and ribbons to an unembellished wreath. Securely hang one half wreath on each door so the two halves meet in the center when the doors are closed. Frame the entrance with a garland and pots of greenery. Place tall topiary forms in the pots for a dramatic addition.

Cottage Christmas

Play up your home's unique style with holiday decorations that complement its most appealing qualities. Boost the charm using objects that share a common look, like the garden-inspired pieces pictured on these pages that work together to convey a cozy welcome. Rustic aluminum containers on the door, porch, and stairs offer casual appeal in keeping with the relaxed architecture. Fill planters with herbs, and use bright accents, such as red amaryllis blooms, berries, ornaments, and gardening accessories, to cheer a neutral setting.

To keep the bucket decoration on the front door fresh, line the bucket with a zip-top plastic freezer bag, then fill it with moistened floral foam. Stick berry stems and evergreen cuttings into the foam. In addition to prolonging the life of the arrangement, the foam makes arranging easier because it holds the pieces in place.

Arrange a collection of similarly themed accent pieces at your front entry to set a welcoming stage for holiday visitors.

Rich in Tradition

Nothing shows off the deep colors of a fresh evergreen garland and wreath better than a pristine white door. Tie on extra-wide red ribbons as accents, and you're all set. If you're in the mood for a bit more embellishment, add twinkling lights to the garland, and set a conifer surrounded by holly berries in a pretty container.

Big lanterns filled with candles are a quick way to spread good cheer to a covered entrance. Consider using flameless candles as a worry-free alternative to regular pillars.

Wreath of Good Fortune
Bells are thought to attract good luck and bring
prosperity, and what better way to greet the season?
This temple-bell wreath starts with a green extruded
craft foam wreath form, which is more dense than
the usual craft foam and better supports the bells.

Here's How

Use U-shaped floral pins to attach reindeer moss to the top and sides of the wreath form. Cut enough short lengths of ribbon to encircle the wreath. Fold lengths in half and pin around the outside edge of the wreath. Loop long ribbons around the bottom of the wreath. Tie bells at the ends of the ribbons.

Natural materials make beautiful and inexpensive Christmas decorations. Combine them with potted plants, ribbons, and other holiday accessories, such as candles and ornaments, to enjoy all season long.

Evergreen Greetings

Top off a square mailbox with an abundant bouquet of winter plants. This mailbox has a convenient planting space at the top, but the idea translates well for any flat surface. Fill a wide, shallow planter with a mix of winter-hardy plants. Tuck in ornaments and oversized pinecones to add color and fill in gaps. Center the container on the top of the mailbox.

A Little Extra

Let an existing mailbox planting be the starting point for a festive presentation. For a mailbox with a post that extends above the box, loosely wrap sheer ribbon around a pine garland and drape the garland around the mailbox. Use wire to hold the garland in place. Wire clusters of bright nandina berries to the top of the post and finish with a big bow for an eye-catching flourish.

Wrapped and Ready

Encircle a traditional mailbox/lamppost with a pine garland, securing it to the post with wire. Wire magnolia leaves and apples to the garland. Use floral picks with wires to secure the apples. Wire or tie loopy bows beneath the lantern to form an ornate collar.

MERRY MANTEL *Decorations*

A toasty, crackling fire makes the fireplace a natural gathering spot during the holidays. On these pages, you'll find ways to decorate this favorite place with festive and welcoming charm.

Foresty Flair

For a beautiful mantel arrangement, start with a good plan in mind. This mantel, decorated with silvery accessories and shimmery white accents, evokes the image of a snow-sprinkled enchanted forest. To create the look, use botanical-themed pieces such as bark candles and pinecones. The ones used on this mantel have a metallic sheen and blend easily with the frosty tree candles and looped chenille stem Christmas tree. Fill in along the mantel with silver ornaments and sprigs of seeded eucalyptus and green berries. Add height with pieces such as the silver angel and the mercury glass vase filled with flowers. Finish the decoration with velvety, moss-colored stockings to complement the woodsy motif.

Windows of Opportunity

Chances are your mantel doesn't have eight cubbyholes to decorate, but the unusual design of the mantelpiece pictured here offers a wealth of holiday decorating ideas that can be used in a variety of places throughout the home. For example, start with a favorite collection, such as transferware china, majolica pieces, and apothecary bottles. Fill bowls, cups, and pitchers with holly and evergreens. Tie little presents with pretty ribbons, and place them among the greenery clippings (above). Create an interesting multi-layered look with stacked cups and saucers, books, and plates on stands. Fill stockings with small packages, berries, and big bows to give a bountifully festive appearance (right).

Use small items, such as tiny bottles, pinecones, ornaments, and wrapped packages, to fill in and add color to the arrangement.

Frame It

These open-frame stocking holders are a perfect way to show off pretty cups and ornaments. Add a posy of berries to embellish a plain ornament.

Three Times as Charming

This trio of sparkling wreaths has a dramatic presence yet is simple to create. Loop a length of wide ribbon around each wreath, and attach to the wall with a small tack. Hang a large, flat ornament, such as a snowflake, in the center of each wreath by threading ribbon through the ornament hanger and tacking the ribbon to the wall behind the wreath. Finish this arrangement by scattering votive candles and boxwood clippings on the mantel top, framing them with silver finials. Go all out with a boxwood garland and dangling silver ornaments attached underneath the mantel.

Back to Nature

Natural materials are second to none when it comes to seasonal decorating. Whether it's fresh flowers or evergreen clippings, you won't go wrong basing your holiday designs on an all-natural scheme.

For an all-green extravaganza, start with a mixed greenery garland that's long enough to trail across the mantel and down both sides (above). Wire or tuck in other naturals, such as magnolia clippings, twigs, pinecones, and artichokes to boost the abundant look.

For a fresh-flower mantel arrangement, select a long, rectangular container that will fit easily on the mantel (right). Fill the container with moistened floral foam, then arrange the flowers. When the flowers fade, replace them with greenery sprigs.

Use fresh materials for decorations that will give you both the look and the fragrances of the holiday season.

Elfin Whimsy

A sweet pair of embroidered elves adorn linen stockings and are joined by more spritely folk perched on top of the mantel. These little elves are easy to embroider and are charming on stockings, as well as on tote bags, tablecloths, napkins, and pillowcases. See page 171 for information on where to find the free elf patterns created by Hillary Lang. Use transfer paper and a ballpoint pen to transfer the design onto the piece you will be embroidering. Look for transfer paper at crafts stores.

Sew Sparkly

Stitch the elf design with metallic embroidery floss to add a glistening sheen. Metallic floss is available in many colors and has reflective qualities that are perfect for embroidered holiday designs.

Flying Colors

Dress your mantel with a colorful pennant garland that's "sew" easy and is a great use for fabric remnants. To make the garland, cut triangles from fabric. The number of flags you'll need depends on where you'll be hanging the garland. With wrong sides facing, stitch two triangles together along the long edges of each triangle. Trim the stitched edges with pinking shears. Stitch the pennants to double fold bias tape (such as quilt binding) or ribbon folded in half lengthwise. Leave a few inches of bias tape on each end for tying. Sew covered buttons between the pennants.

Cut pennants from a variety of fabric designs for a lively garland to hang on a mantel, a doorway, or a window.

Here's How
Use pinking shears to give a decorative finish to the fabric triangles. It also will prevent the fabric from raveling.

Bottle Brigade

There's strength in numbers and plenty of panache, too, as this collection of bottles proves. Arrange an assortment of new and vintage bottles and jars along the mantel. Use ornaments and greenery, such as seeded eucalyptus, to add seasonal color. For a finishing touch, fill clear globe ornaments with tiny ornaments and sprigs and hang them with ribbons from the mantel.

KITCHEN *Accents*

It's the heart of the home and the favorite gathering spot when friends and family get together, so give the kitchen the attention it deserves when it's time to decorate for the holiday season. Here are some fresh ideas.

Tool Time

Search the kitchen cabinets and drawers for cute cooking implements, and arrange them on the countertop for an unexpected seasonal decoration. Silver mixing bowls, cake pans, and measuring cups look especially festive when paired with bright red bowls and baking tools.

Add a touch of green with potted plants, such as rosemary, parsley, and tiny cedar trees. Fill in with fresh fruits and flowers in shades of red, green, and white. To add pizzazz to the display, use wire racks and cake stands to vary the heights of the pieces.

Hang It Up
Deck the walls with a tree-shaped display of Christmas plates. Use wire plate hangers, or, for invisible hangers, use adhesive-backed plate hangers that stick to the backs of the plates. The adhesive hangers are less likely to scratch or chip the plates and are easily removed by soaking the plates in warm water.

Dress the kitchen window with a
jaunty garland made by stringing petite
packages on a shiny cord.

Flame On

Beautiful soup ladles are naturals for trimming the kitchen mantel. Use long ribbons to tie the ladles to stocking holders. Add a warm glow by placing flameless tea lights in the ladles.

Flameless candles are the key to this glowing arrangement. They're widely available at crafts and discount stores.

Herbal Essence

A bay leaf wreath and garland are ideal holiday decorations for the kitchen. Bay leaves are long lasting, dry beautifully, and can be harvested for cooking.

Pump up the charm by adding a fragrant herb swag to the wreath. To make an herb swag, clip stems of a variety of herbs that dry well, such as rosemary, bay, and lavender. Tie the stems together with raffia, then tie or wire to the bay wreath.

Drape a kitchen doorway with a bay leaf garland to extend the theme into an adjoining room.

BAKE A BATCH OF BIG FAT COOKIES, A GLISTENING TURKEY FOR THE HOLIDAY PLATTER, A TASTY CHICKEN CASSEROLE FOR A CROWD, OR A MAGICAL DESSERT FROM CAKE MIX. TURN THE PAGE, AND YOU CAN HAVE IT ALL.

Recipes

Red Velvet Cookies With
Cream Cheese Frosting

BIG FAT *Cookies*

Cookies are quite possibly the premier food of the holiday season. This selection is no less than stellar, both in ultimate flavor and awesome appearance.

editor's favorite • make ahead

Red Velvet Cookies With Cream Cheese Frosting

Red Velvet is a tradition in the South, and these cookies are every bit as good as the time-honored cake.

Prep: 35 min. Cook: 15 min. per batch Other: 25 min.

2¾   cups all-purpose flour
⅓   cup unsweetened cocoa
1½   tsp. baking powder
½   tsp. baking soda
¼   tsp. salt
1   cup butter, softened
1¼   cups sugar
2   large eggs
2   Tbsp. red liquid food coloring
1   Tbsp. vanilla extract
¾   cup buttermilk
Parchment paper
Cream Cheese Frosting

Preheat oven to 350°. Combine first 5 ingredients in a medium bowl.

Beat butter at medium speed with an electric mixer 2 minutes or until creamy. Gradually add sugar, beating well. Add eggs, 1 at a time, beating until blended after each addition. Beat in food coloring and vanilla.

Add flour mixture alternately with buttermilk, beginning and ending with flour mixture. Beat at low speed until blended after each addition, stopping to scrape bowl as needed.

Drop dough by ¼ cupfuls 3" apart onto parchment paper-lined baking sheets. Spread dough to 3" rounds.

Bake at 350° for 15 minutes or until tops are set. Cool on baking sheets 5 minutes. Remove to wire racks, and cool completely (about 20 minutes). Crumble 1 cookie into fine crumbs to use as garnish. Spread about 2½ Tbsp. Cream Cheese Frosting onto each cookie; sprinkle with

crumbs. Store cookies in refrigerator up to 5 days. **Yield: 20 cookies.**

Cream Cheese Frosting:

Prep: 4 min.
1   (8-oz.) package cream cheese, softened
½   cup butter, softened
½   teaspoon vanilla extract
Dash of salt
1   (1-lb.) box powdered sugar

Beat cream cheese, butter, vanilla, and salt at medium speed with an electric mixer 1 minute or until creamy. Gradually add powered sugar, beating at low speed 2 minutes or until smooth. **Yield: 3 cups.**

For an attractive topping, crumble one cookie and use the crumbs as garnish.

Ginger Giants

These puffy, sugar-crusted cookies have crunchy edges and soft centers.

Prep: 15 min. Cook: 16 min. per batch Other: 2 hr., 10 min.

¾ cup butter, softened
1 cup firmly packed light brown sugar
1 large egg
⅓ cup molasses
1 tsp. vanilla extract
2¼ cups all-purpose flour
2 Tbsp. ground ginger
2 tsp. baking soda
1½ tsp. ground cinnamon
1 tsp. ground cloves
½ tsp. salt
½ cup turbinado sugar
Parchment paper

Beat butter at medium speed with an electric mixer until creamy. Gradually add brown sugar, beating until fluffy. Add egg, molasses, and vanilla, beating until blended.

Combine flour and next 5 ingredients; gradually add to butter mixture, beating just until blended after each addition. Cover and chill dough 2 hours or overnight.

Preheat oven to 350°. Divide dough into 12 (¼-cup) portions; shape each portion into a ball. Place turbinado sugar in a small bowl; roll each dough ball in sugar. Place balls 2" apart on parchment paper-lined baking sheets. Chill 10 to 15 minutes.

Bake at 350° for 14 to 16 minutes or until edges are lightly browned; cool on baking sheets 5 minutes. Remove to wire racks. **Yield: 1 dozen.**

Note: If you chill dough overnight, let it stand at room temperature about 15 minutes or until it becomes pliable.

Chocolate Chip Brownie Pillows

These are gargantuan cookies, each with a fudgy brownie "pillow" in the middle. You'll have extra brownies leftover to enjoy right away or to freeze.

**Prep: 32 min. Cook: 40 min., plus 20 min. per batch
Other: 1 hr., 17 min.**

1 (20-oz.) package double chocolate brownie mix (we tested with Ghirardelli)
½ cup unsalted butter, softened
½ cup butter-flavored shortening
1½ cups firmly packed brown sugar
2 large eggs
1 egg yolk
1 Tbsp. vanilla extract
2½ cups unbleached all-purpose flour
2 tsp. baking powder
½ tsp. baking soda
½ tsp. salt
3 cups semisweet chocolate morsels
Parchment paper

Preheat oven to 325°. Prepare and bake brownie mix according to package directions in an 8" square pan. Let cool completely in pan on a wire rack. Cut brownies into 3 dozen squares.

Beat butter and shortening at medium speed with an electric mixer until creamy. Add brown sugar, beating until smooth. Add eggs, egg yolk, and vanilla, beating until blended.

Combine flour and next 3 ingredients; gradually add to butter mixture, beating just until blended after each addition. Stir in chocolate morsels. Cover and chill dough 1 hour.

Increase oven temperature to 350°. For each cookie, scoop a level ½ cup dough onto parchment paper-lined baking sheets; place cookies 3" apart. Using your fingers, make an indentation in mound of dough; place 1 brownie square in center. Press chocolate chip dough around brownie, reshaping dough to form a ball. Repeat procedure with remaining dough and 10 brownie squares, placing no more than 6 cookies on a baking sheet. Chill 15 minutes.

Bake at 350° for 18 to 20 minutes or until lightly browned and cookies look set. Cool 2 minutes on baking sheets; remove to wire racks, and cool completely. **Yield: 11 cookies.**

Chocolate Chip Brownie
Pillows

Place a brownie bite in middle of each dough mound.

Shape cookie dough around brownie, covering it completely.

Orange-Frosted Cornmeal
Stars

Orange-Frosted Cornmeal Stars

Prep: 29 min.   Cook: 14 min. per batch   Other: 55 min.

1   cup butter, softened
1   cup granulated sugar
2   egg whites
1   egg yolk
2   Tbsp. orange zest, divided
5   Tbsp. fresh orange juice, divided
1½   tsp. vanilla extract
2¾   cups all-purpose flour
⅔   cup yellow cornmeal
1½   tsp. baking powder
½   tsp. salt
Parchment paper
2   cups powdered sugar

Beat butter and granulated sugar at medium speed with an electric mixer until fluffy. In a separate bowl, beat egg whites at high speed until stiff peaks form; add to butter mixture, beating just until blended. Add egg yolk, 1½ Tbsp. orange zest, 2 Tbsp. orange juice, and vanilla, beating just until blended.

Combine flour and next 3 ingredients; gradually add to butter mixture, beating just until blended after each addition.

Shape dough into a ball, and divide in half. Flatten each half into a 5" disk; wrap each disk in plastic wrap. Freeze dough 30 minutes, or chill 8 hours.

Preheat oven to 350°. Roll out dough, 1 portion at a time, to ¼" thickness on a floured surface; cut into star shapes using a 4" or 5" star-shaped cutter. Reroll trimmings to make additional cookies. Place cutouts 1" apart on parchment paper-lined baking sheets.

Bake at 350° for 14 minutes or until golden. Cool 5 minutes on baking sheets; remove to wire racks, and cool completely (about 20 minutes).

Combine remaining ½ Tbsp. orange zest, remaining 3 Tbsp. orange juice, and powdered sugar in a medium bowl, stirring with a whisk until smooth. Spread frosting on stars. Place cookies on wire racks until frosting is set. **Yield: 20 cookies.**

Walnut Scotchies

Gobble these crisp, butterscotch-flavored cookies up plain, or slather ice cream between pairs of them to make irresistible mega sandwich cookies.

Prep: 20 min.   Cook: 24 min. per batch   Other: 5 min.

1½   cups coarsely chopped walnuts
2   cups all-purpose flour
1   tsp. baking soda
¼   tsp. salt
½   cup butter, softened
¾   cup granulated sugar
½   cup firmly packed light brown sugar
2   large eggs
1   tsp. vanilla extract
1   cup butterscotch morsels
Parchment paper

Preheat oven to 350°. Place walnuts in a single layer in a shallow pan. Bake at 350° for 6 to 8 minutes until toasted and fragrant. Cool.

Process ½ cup toasted walnuts in a food processor until finely ground; place in a medium bowl. Add flour, baking soda, and salt to ground nuts, stirring well with a whisk.

Beat butter at medium speed with an electric mixer until creamy. Gradually add sugars, beating until light and fluffy; beat in eggs and vanilla. Gradually add flour mixture, beating at low speed until blended after each addition. Stir in butterscotch morsels and remaining 1 cup toasted walnuts.

Drop dough by level ¼ cupfuls onto parchment paper-lined baking sheets. (Do not flatten.)

Bake at 350° for 16 minutes or until edges are lightly browned. Cool on baking sheets 5 minutes. Remove to wire racks, and cool completely. **Yield: 16 cookies.**

Walnut Scotchie Ice Cream Sandwiches: Spread about ⅓ cup slightly softened premium vanilla ice cream onto flat side of 1 cookie. Top with another cookie; gently press together. Wrap in plastic wrap and freeze, or enjoy right away. Repeat with remaining cookies and additional ice cream. **Yield: 8 sandwiches.**

Toffee-Pecan Cookies

For maximum chunkiness in your cookies, break toffee bars and pecan halves by hand to get big pieces.

**Prep: 27 min.   Cook: 7 min., plus 17 min. per batch
Other: 2 min.**

1	cup pecan halves, broken in half
2	cups all-purpose flour
1	tsp. baking soda
¼	tsp. salt
6	Tbsp. butter, softened
6	Tbsp. shortening
¾	cup granulated sugar
½	cup firmly packed brown sugar
1	large egg
1	tsp. vanilla extract
6	(1.4-oz.) chocolate-covered toffee candy bars, coarsely broken (we tested with SKOR)

Parchment paper

Preheat oven to 350°. Place pecans in a single layer in a shallow pan. Bake at 350° for 7 minutes or until toasted and fragrant; cool.

Stir together flour, baking soda, and salt in a medium bowl.

Beat butter and shortening at medium speed with an electric mixer until creamy. Gradually add sugars, beating until smooth. Add egg and vanilla, beating until blended. Gradually add flour mixture, beating just until blended after each addition. Stir in pecans and toffee bars.

Drop dough by ¼ cupfuls 2" to 3" apart onto parchment paper-lined baking sheets.

Bake at 350° for 17 minutes or until edges are lightly browned. Cool on baking sheets 2 minutes. Remove to wire racks, and cool completely. **Yield: 16 cookies.**

Cornmeal-Almond Cookies

This unique cookie earned our Test Kitchens' highest rating for its texture: a chewiness from the almond paste and a delicate crunch from the cornmeal.

Prep: 39 min.   Cook: 18 min. per batch   Other: 2 hr., 5 min.

1	cup all-purpose flour
1	cup yellow cornmeal
1½	tsp. baking powder
¼	tsp. salt
¾	cup butter, softened
1	(7-oz.) package almond paste, crumbled
1	cup sugar
2	egg whites
1	Tbsp. orange zest
1	tsp. vanilla extract
1	cup sliced almonds, coarsely chopped

Parchment paper

Combine flour and next 3 ingredients in a medium bowl.

Beat butter at medium speed with an electric mixer until creamy. Gradually add almond paste; beat until smooth. Gradually add sugar, beating until combined. Add egg whites, orange zest, and vanilla; beat until blended. Gradually add flour mixture; beat at low speed just until blended after each addition. Shape dough into a ball, wrap in plastic wrap, and chill 2 hours or until firm.

Preheat oven to 350°. Place almonds in a shallow bowl. Shape dough by ¼ cupfuls into balls; roll each ball in almonds to coat. Place balls 3" apart on parchment paper-lined baking sheets.

Bake at 350° for 18 minutes or until edges are lightly browned. Cool on baking sheets 5 minutes. Remove to wire racks, and cool completely. **Yield: 13 cookies.**

Toffee-Pecan Cookies

German Chocolate
Cake Cookies

German Chocolate Cake Cookies

The flavor of these cookies is reminiscent of the classic German chocolate layer cake.

Prep: 14 min.   Cook: 18 min. per batch   Other: 25 min.

¾   cup unsalted butter, softened
¾   cup granulated sugar
¼   cup firmly packed light brown sugar
1   large egg
2   tsp. light corn syrup
2   tsp. vanilla extract
¼   tsp. coconut extract
2   cups all-purpose flour
1   tsp. baking powder
¼   tsp. salt
3   (1-oz.) German chocolate baking squares, melted
1   cup chopped pecans, toasted
½   cup semisweet chocolate chunks
½   cup unsweetened organic coconut flakes or sweetened flaked coconut
1½ cups powdered sugar
2   Tbsp. milk
¼   tsp. vanilla extract
1   cup sweetened flaked coconut (we tested with Mounds)

Preheat oven to 350°. Beat butter and granulated and brown sugars at medium speed with an electric mixer until blended. Add egg, corn syrup, 2 tsp. vanilla extract, and coconut extract, beating until blended.

Combine flour, baking powder, and salt; gradually add to butter mixture, beating just until blended after each addition. Stir in melted chocolate and next 3 ingredients.

Drop dough by ¼ cupfuls 2" apart onto lightly greased baking sheets.

Bake at 350° for 16 to 18 minutes. Cool 5 minutes on baking sheets; remove to wire racks, and cool completely (about 20 minutes).

Whisk together powdered sugar, milk, and ¼ vanilla in a small bowl until smooth. Spoon icing over cookies; immediately sprinkle with sweetened flaked coconut.
Yield: 15 cookies.

Note: Find unsweetened organic coconut flakes in your local specialty food market.

Oatmeal Cookie Sandwiches
With Rum-Raisin Filling

editor's favorite • gift idea

Oatmeal Cookie Sandwiches With Rum-Raisin Filling

A creamy rum-flavored filling glues these oversized oatmeal cookies together.

Prep: 50 min.   Cook: 12 min. per batch   Other: 23 min.

½   cup butter, softened
½   cup shortening
¼   cup light corn syrup
1¼   cups firmly packed light brown sugar
1   large egg
1½   tsp. almond extract
1½   cups all-purpose flour
1   tsp. baking soda
1   tsp. ground cinnamon
½   tsp. salt
½   tsp. ground cloves
2   cups uncooked regular oats
¾   cup chopped pecans
Parchment paper
Rum-Raisin Filling

Preheat oven to 375°. Beat first 4 ingredients at medium speed with an electric mixer until fluffy. Add egg and almond extract, beating until blended.

Whisk together flour, baking soda, and next 3 ingredients in a medium bowl; gradually add to butter mixture, beating at low speed until blended after each addition. Stir in oats and pecans.

Shape dough into 1½" balls. Place balls 2" apart on large parchment paper-lined baking sheets.

Bake at 375° for 10 to 12 minutes or until golden. Cool on baking sheets 3 minutes. Remove to wire racks, and cool completely (about 20 minutes). Spread about 3 Tbsp. Rum-Raisin Filling onto each of half the cookies; top with remaining cookies. **Yield: 15 sandwiches.**

Rum-Raisin Filling:

Prep: 10 min.

1   (3-oz.) package cream cheese, softened
3   Tbsp. milk
1   Tbsp. dark rum*
¾   tsp. vanilla extract
⅛   tsp. salt
1   (1-lb.) package powdered sugar
1½   cups raisins

Beat cream cheese at medium speed with an electric mixer until creamy. Add milk and next 3 ingredients, beating until blended. Gradually add powdered sugar, beating at low speed until smooth. Stir in raisins. **Yield: 2½ cups.**

*Omit rum, if desired.

editor's favorite • gift idea

Chunky Chocolate-White Chocolate-Espresso Cookies

If you're in for an amazingly good drop cookie, these thick cookies with soft white chocolate and a hint of coffee really hit the spot.

Prep: 14 min.   Cook: 21 min. per batch   Other: 5 min.

¾   cup butter, softened
1½   cups sugar
2   large eggs
1   tsp. vanilla extract
2   (3.5-oz.) dark chocolate bars with finely ground espresso beans, divided and chopped (we tested with Ghirardelli Espresso Escape)
2¼   cups all-purpose flour
¼   cup cocoa
½   tsp. baking soda
¼   tsp. salt
2   (4-oz.) white chocolate bars, chopped (we tested with Ghirardelli)
1   cup coarsely chopped pecan halves, toasted

Preheat oven to 350°. Beat butter and sugar at medium speed with an electric mixer until blended. Add eggs and vanilla, beating just until blended. Microwave half of dark chocolate in a small, microwave-safe bowl at HIGH 50 seconds to 1 minute or until melted, stirring after 30 seconds. Add melted chocolate to butter mixture, beating just until blended.

Combine flour and next 3 ingredients; gradually add to butter mixture, beating just until blended after each addition. Stir in remaining dark chocolate, white chocolate, and pecans.

Drop dough by ⅓ cupfuls 2" apart onto lightly greased baking sheets.

Bake at 350° for 21 minutes. Cool on baking sheets 5 minutes. Remove to wire racks, and cool completely. **Yield: 15 cookies.**

Chunky Chocolate-White Chocolate-Espresso Cookies

Toffee-Tiramisù Layer Cake

CAKE MIX *Magic*

Using cake mix with these impressive yet easy dessert ideas makes the holidays just a bit more relaxed.

editor's favorite • make ahead

Toffee-Tiramisù Layer Cake

Just like traditional Tiramisù, this towering cake is best when made ahead so the flavors can meld. Our Test Kitchens staff gave this dessert our highest rating.

Prep: 27 min.   Cook: 30 min.   Other: 16 hr.

Wax paper
1   (18.25-oz.) package French vanilla cake mix
    (we tested with Pillsbury)
1   (1.16-oz.) package Swiss mocha cappuccino mix
    (we tested with Land O'Lakes)
⅓   cup vegetable oil
3   large eggs
¾   cup Cinnamon-Espresso Syrup
Mascarpone Frosting
3   (1.4-oz) chocolate-covered toffee candy bars,
    chopped (we tested with SKOR)
Garnishes: additional chopped chocolate-covered
    toffee candy bars, semisweet chocolate and white
    chocolate shavings

Preheat oven to 350°. Lightly grease 2 (8") round cake pans; line with wax paper. Lightly grease wax paper. Dust pans with flour; shake out excess, and set aside.

Beat cake mix, next 3 ingredients, and 1 cup water in a large bowl at low speed with an electric mixer 30 seconds; then beat at medium speed 2 minutes. Pour batter into prepared pans.

Bake at 350° for 28 to 30 minutes or until a wooden pick inserted in center comes out clean. Let cool in pans on wire racks 10 minutes; remove from pans. Discard wax paper, and cool layers completely on wire racks (1 hour). Wrap and chill cake layers 1 to 24 hours. (This step enables you to split layers with ease.)

Using a serrated knife, slice layers in half horizontally to make 4 layers. Place 1 layer, cut side up, on a cake plate. Brush with one-fourth of Cinnamon-Espresso Syrup. Spread with 1½ cups Mascarpone Frosting; sprinkle with one-fourth chopped chocolate-covered toffee pieces. Repeat process with remaining 3 layers, syrup, frosting, and chopped candy bar. Frost sides of cake with remaining 2½ cups frosting. Garnish, if desired. Cover and refrigerate overnight. Store in refrigerator. **Yield: 12 servings.**

Cinnamon-Espresso Syrup:

Prep: 2 min.   Cook: 4 min.   Other: 15 min.

⅔   cup sugar
1   (3") cinnamon stick, broken in half
1   Tbsp. instant espresso powder
¼   cup coffee liqueur

Bring 1 cup water, sugar, and cinnamon stick to a boil in a small saucepan; boil 1 minute. Remove from heat; let stand 15 minutes. Remove and discard cinnamon stick. Stir in espresso powder and liqueur. **Yield: about 1¼ cups.**

Mascarpone Frosting:

Prep: 13 min.

2   (8-oz.) containers mascarpone cheese
1   cup powdered sugar
2   tsp. vanilla extract
½   cup Cinnamon-Espresso Syrup
2½ cups whipping cream, whipped

Beat first 3 ingredients at low speed with an electric mixer until creamy. Gradually add Cinnamon-Espresso Syrup, beating until smooth. Fold in whipped cream. Cover and chill until ready to use. **Yield: 8½ cups.**

Gingerbread Cupcakes With Lemon Curd and Vanilla Bean Cream

Just the aroma of these little ginger cakes baking will put you in the Christmas spirit.

Prep: 16 min.   Cook: 18 min.   Other: 45 min.

1   (14.5-oz.) package gingerbread cake and cookie
       mix (we tested with Betty Crocker)
1   large egg
1   tsp. lemon zest
Paper baking cups
Lemon Curd, chilled
Vanilla Bean Cream

Preheat oven to 350°. Beat cake mix, 1¼ cups water, egg, and lemon zest at medium speed with an electric mixer 1 minute or until well blended.

Place baking cups in standard muffin pans; spoon batter into cups, filling two-thirds full.

Bake at 350° for 18 minutes or until a wooden pick inserted in center comes out clean. Remove from pans to wire racks, and cool completely (about 45 minutes).

Snip 1 corner of a zip-top plastic freezer bag to fit a No. 10 metal pastry tip. Insert tip into hole in bag. Fill bag with Lemon Curd. Use pastry tip to poke a hole in top of each cupcake. Squeeze about 1 Tbsp. curd into each cupcake. Frost cupcakes with Vanilla Bean Cream. Store in refrigerator. **Yield: 15 cupcakes.**

Lemon Curd:

Prep: 8 min.   Cook: 4 min.   Other: 8 hr.
⅓   cup sugar
2   tsp. lemon zest
⅓   cup fresh lemon juice
2   large eggs, beaten
¼   cup butter, cut into small cubes

Combine first 4 ingredients in a medium saucepan, stirring with a whisk. Add butter, and cook, stirring constantly, over medium-low heat 4 minutes or until thickened. Pour lemon curd through a fine wire-mesh strainer into a medium bowl. Place heavy-duty plastic wrap directly on lemon curd (to prevent a film from forming). Chill at least 8 hours. **Yield: 1 cup.**

Vanilla Bean Cream:

Prep: 2 min.

1   cup heavy whipping cream
½   vanilla bean, split lengthwise
¼   cup sugar

Pour cream into a bowl. Scrape seeds from vanilla bean into cream. Beat whipping cream mixture at low speed until foamy; gradually add sugar, beating at medium speed with an electric mixer until soft peaks form. Chill until ready to use. **Yield: 1¾ cups.**

Walnut-Fig Streusel Bars

Give these fig-rich bars a generous dusting of powdered sugar for a pretty appearance.

Prep: 12 min.   Cook: 45 min.

1   (18-oz.) package butter pecan cake mix
       (we tested with Betty Crocker)
2   cups uncooked regular oats
1½   cups chopped walnuts
1   cup butter, melted
½   cup firmly packed dark brown sugar
1   large egg
2   (8.5-oz.) jars fig spread (we tested with
       Dalmatia Fig Spread)
2   tsp. orange zest
Powdered sugar (optional)

Preheat oven to 350°. Combine first 6 ingredients in a large bowl. Beat at low speed with an electric mixer until blended. Reserve 1½ cups oat mixture for streusel topping. Press remaining oat mixture into bottom of a lightly greased 9" square pan.

Bake at 350° for 18 minutes or until crust begins to brown.

Stir together fig spread and orange zest in a small bowl. Pour filling over crust. Crumble reserved oat topping over filling.

Bake at 350° for 30 minutes or until browned. Cool completely in pan on a wire rack. Cut into bars, and, if desired, sprinkle with powdered sugar. **Yield: 20 bars.**

Note: Find fig spread at upscale markets such as Whole Foods or Cost Plus World Market or online at www.VermontCountryStore.com

Lane Cake

Dried cherries, bittersweet chocolate, and the simplicity of starting with a cake mix give this Southern cake new appeal.

Prep: 19 min.   Cook: 14 min.   Other: 1 hr. 10 min.

4   egg whites
1   (18.25-oz.) package white cake mix
    (we tested with Duncan Hines)
1   cup sour cream
⅓   cup unsalted butter, melted
2   tsp. vanilla extract
Parchment paper
Bourbon Filling
Fluff Frosting

Preheat oven to 350°. Beat egg whites in a medium-size mixing bowl at high speed with an electric mixer until stiff peaks form.

Combine cake mix and next 3 ingredients in a large mixing bowl; add ¼ cup water. Beat at low speed 30 seconds; beat at medium speed 2 minutes, scraping down sides, if necessary. Fold in beaten egg whites.

Pour batter into 3 greased and floured, parchment paper-lined 9" round cake pans.

Bake at 350° for 14 minutes or until a wooden pick inserted in center comes out clean. Let cool in pans on wire racks 10 minutes; remove from pans, and cool completely on wire racks (1 hour).

Place 1 layer on a cake plate. Spread with 1½ cups Bourbon Filling. Repeat procedure with remaining 2 layers and Bourbon Filling (ending with remaining filling on top). Frost sides of cake with Fluff Frosting. Cover and chill cake until ready to serve. **Yield: 12 servings.**

Bourbon Filling:

Prep: 12 min.   Cook: 28 min.   Other: 5 hr.

12   egg yolks
1½   cups sugar
¾   cup unsalted butter, melted
½   cup bourbon
1½   tsp. vanilla extract
1½   cups finely chopped pecans
1½   cups coarsely chopped dried cherries
1½   cups sweetened flaked coconut
1   (4-oz.) bittersweet chocolate baking bar, chopped

Beat egg yolks in a large glass or metal bowl at medium speed with an electric mixer 3 minutes; gradually add sugar, beating until blended. Beat 3 minutes. Gradually add butter; beat at low speed until blended.

Pour water to a depth of 1" in a saucepan over medium heat; bring water to a boil. Reduce heat to a simmer. Place egg yolk mixture in bowl over simmering water. Cook, stirring constantly, 28 minutes or until an instant-read thermometer registers 190°. Remove from heat; stir in bourbon and vanilla. Add pecans, cherries, and coconut, stirring well. Let cool completely. Cover and chill 4 hours. Gently fold in chocolate. **Yield: about 5 cups.**

Fluff Frosting:

Prep: 5 min.

1   cup unsalted butter, softened
1   (7-oz.) jar marshmallow crème
2   tsp. vanilla extract
1   cup powdered sugar

Beat butter in a large mixing bowl at medium speed with an electric mixer until creamy. Add marshmallow crème and vanilla, beating until blended. Add powdered sugar; beat at high speed 3 minutes or until fluffy, scraping down sides. **Yield: about 2⅓ cups.**

Lane Cake

Dark Chocolate-Peppermint
Baby Cakes

make ahead

Dark Chocolate-Peppermint Baby Cakes

Transform simple cake mix into petits fours drenched with a silky chocolate frosting called ganache. Take advantage of the make-ahead steps to simplify assembly.

Prep: 1 hr., 18 min.   Cook: 45 min.   Other: 9 hr., 56 min.

1   (18.25-oz.) package devil's food cake mix
        (we tested with Duncan Hines)
½   cup vegetable oil
3   large eggs
3½   cups heavy whipping cream, divided
1   cup finely crushed peppermint candies (about 26)
1   tsp. peppermint extract, divided
8   oz. white chocolate morsels (about 1⅓ cups)
¼   cup light corn syrup
6   (4-oz.) bittersweet chocolate baking bars, chopped
¼   cup butter, cut into pieces
Wax paper
Garnish: coarsely crushed peppermint candy

Preheat oven to 350°. Grease and flour a 13" x 9" pan. Prepare cake mix according to package directions, using 1⅓ cups water, vegetable oil, and eggs. Pour batter into prepared pan.

Bake at 350° for 35 minutes or until a wooden pick inserted in center comes out clean. Let cool in pan on a wire rack 15 minutes. Remove from pan, and cool completely on wire rack.

While cake cools, heat 1½ cups cream, 1 cup crushed peppermints, and ½ teaspoon peppermint extract in a saucepan over medium heat, stirring occasionally, just until bubbles appear (do not boil). Pour hot cream mixture through a fine wire-mesh strainer over white chocolate in a bowl, discarding any undissolved peppermints. Let stand 1 minute; stir until smooth. Cover and chill 8 hours.

Wrap cake and chill 8 hours. (This step enables you to split cake with ease.)

Beat chilled peppermint-white chocolate mixture at high speed with an electric mixer until light and fluffy.

Using a serrated knife, slice cake horizontally into 3 layers. Place 1 cake layer on a large cutting board; spread with half of peppermint filling. Top with second cake layer. Spread with remaining peppermint filling. Top with remaining cake layer. Cover and freeze 1 hour.

Trim and discard ½" from all sides of cake. Cut trimmed cake into 24 squares. Place cake squares in freezer for 30 minutes.

Meanwhile, heat remaining 2 cups whipping cream, corn syrup, and remaining ½ teaspoon peppermint extract in a saucepan over medium heat just until bubbles appear (do not boil). Pour hot cream mixture over chopped bittersweet chocolate. Let stand 1 minute; stir until smooth. Gradually stir in butter until blended. Let ganache stand 10 minutes.

Place cakes, 6 at a time, on a wire rack over wax paper. Using a small spatula, spread ganache on sides and tops of cakes. Repeat procedure with remaining cakes and ganache. Garnish, if desired. Chill at least 30 minutes or until ganache is firm. **Yield: 2 dozen.**

Note: To save half the recipe for another time, wrap and store 12 filled cakes in freezer up to 2 weeks. Cover and chill half of ganache in refrigerator. Microwave ganache at MEDIUM 4 minutes, stirring after 2 minutes. Stir until smooth. Spread ganache on cakes as above.

An offset spatula makes spreading the ganache easier, but any small spatula will do the job.

Pumpkin Spice Bars

make ahead

Pumpkin Spice Bars

Spice cake mix serves double duty as the crust and topping.

Prep: 12 min. Cook: 45 min. Other: 40 min.

1	(18.25-oz.) package spice cake mix (we tested with Duncan Hines)
½	cup butter, melted
½	cup finely chopped pecans
1	Tbsp. vanilla extract
1	(8-oz.) package cream cheese, softened
⅓	cup firmly packed light brown sugar
1	cup canned unsweetened pumpkin
1	large egg
1	tsp. vanilla extract
½	cup finely chopped white chocolate
1	Tbsp. butter, melted
⅓	cup uncooked regular oats

Powdered sugar (optional)

Preheat oven to 350°. Combine first 4 ingredients, mixing well with a fork. Reserve 1 cup crumbs for streusel topping. Press remaining crumbs into a lightly greased 13" x 9" pan.

Bake at 350° for 13 to 15 minutes or until puffy and set. Cool in pan on a wire rack 20 minutes.

Beat cream cheese at medium speed with an electric mixer 30 seconds or until creamy. Add brown sugar, pumpkin, egg, and 1 tsp. vanilla; beat until blended. Pour filling over baked crust.

Stir white chocolate, 1 Tbsp. melted butter, and oats into reserved 1 cup streusel. Sprinkle over filling.

Bake at 350° for 30 minutes or until edges begin to brown and center is set. Cool completely in pan on a wire rack. Sprinkle with powdered sugar, if desired. Cut into bars. Serve at room temperature or chilled. **Yield: 2 dozen.**

editor's favorite • *make ahead*

Dark Rum Spice Cake

This moist sweet potato cake tastes even better the second day.

Prep: 19 min. Cook: 40 min. Other: 1 hr. 5 min.

¾	cup pecan halves
1	(15-oz.) can sweet potatoes in syrup, drained
3	large eggs
1	cup sour cream
¼	cup vegetable oil
1	(18.25-oz.) package spice cake mix (we tested with Duncan Hines)
¾	cup firmly packed light brown sugar
¼	cup butter
2	Tbsp. whipping cream
¼	cup dark rum

Powdered sugar

Preheat oven to 350°. Grease and flour a 12-cup Bundt pan (we recommend greasing pan with shortening). Arrange pecan halves in bottom of pan.

Beat sweet potatoes at low speed with an electric mixer until smooth. Add eggs, sour cream, and oil, beating until blended. Add cake mix; beat 1 minute or until blended. Scrape sides of bowl; beat at medium speed 2 minutes. Pour batter into prepared pan.

Bake at 350° for 35 minutes or until a wooden pick inserted in center comes out clean. Cool in pan on a wire rack 5 minutes.

Meanwhile, combine brown sugar, butter, and cream in a small saucepan. Bring to a boil; boil, stirring often, 1 minute or until sugar melts. Remove pan from heat; carefully stir in rum (mixture will start to foam). Pierce cake multiple times using a metal or wooden skewer. Pour rum syrup over cake. Cool cake completely in pan on wire rack.

To serve, invert cake onto a serving platter; sprinkle with powdered sugar. **Yield: 12 servings.**

make ahead
White Christmas Coconut Sheet Cake

Enjoy this portable, moist sheet cake slathered with lemon curd, whipped cream, and plenty of coconut.

Prep: 28 min.   Cook: 36 min.   Other: 10 hr.

1	(18.25-oz.) package white cake mix (we tested with Duncan Hines)
¾	cup cream of coconut
¼	cup unsalted butter, melted
3	large eggs
¾	cup lemon curd (we tested with Dickinson's)
4	oz. white chocolate, chopped
½	cup sour cream
1	cup whipping cream
¼	cup powdered sugar
1	(6-oz.) package frozen grated coconut, thawed

Garnishes: maraschino cherries with stems, lemon zest

Preheat oven to 350°. Combine first 4 ingredients and ½ cup water in a large bowl; beat at low speed with an electric mixer 1 minute. Increase speed to medium, and beat 1½ minutes. Spread batter into a greased and floured 13" x 9" pan.

Bake at 350° for 35 minutes or until a wooden pick inserted in center comes out clean. Remove pan to a wire rack; spread lemon curd over hot cake. Let cool completely in pan on a wire rack. (Cake will sink slightly in center.)

Microwave white chocolate in a small microwave-safe bowl at HIGH 1 minute or until melted, stirring after 30 seconds. Stir in sour cream. Cover and chill 30 minutes.

Beat whipping cream and powdered sugar in a large bowl at medium speed until stiff peaks form. Add white chocolate mixture, and beat at low speed just until combined. Spread whipped cream topping over cake; sprinkle with coconut. Cover and chill 8 hours. Garnish, if desired. Store in refrigerator. **Yield: 15 servings.**

White Christmas Coconut Sheet Cake

Chocolate-Bourbon-Pecan Cake

CHOCOLATE *Heaven*

Chocolate is a given at Christmastime. The options here tease the taste buds for nearly every occasion—breakfast, food gift, fancy dinner, and comfort food.

editor's favorite • make ahead
Chocolate-Bourbon-Pecan Cake

Serve this ultra-Southern cake on the second day, moist and saturated with bourbon flavor.

Prep: 14 min.   Cook: 40 min.   Other: 10 hr., 10 min.

3   cups all-purpose flour
2¼   tsp. baking soda
¾   tsp. salt
1½   cups boiling water
1¼   cups unsweetened cocoa
¾   cup milk
1   Tbsp. vanilla extract
1½   cups unsalted butter, softened
3   cups firmly packed light brown sugar
6   large eggs
½   cup bourbon
Two-Part Frosting
Garnish: pecans

Preheat oven to 350°. Grease and flour 2 (9") round cake pans. Whisk together flour, baking soda, and salt.

Whisk together 1½ cups boiling water and cocoa, whisking until smooth. Whisk in milk and vanilla.

Beat butter at medium speed with an electric mixer until creamy. Gradually add brown sugar, beating at medium speed 3 minutes or until light and fluffy. Add eggs, 1 at a time, beating well after each addition.

With mixer at low speed, add dry ingredients alternately with cocoa mixture, beginning and ending with dry ingredients. Pour batter into prepared pans.

Bake at 350° for 35 to 40 minutes or until a wooden pick inserted in center comes out clean. Let cool in pans on wire racks 10 minutes; remove from pans, and cool completely on wire racks (about 1 hour). Wrap and freeze cake layers 1 hour. (This step enables you to split cake layers with ease.)

Using a serrated knife, slice cake layers in half horizontally to make 4 layers. Brush cut side of each layer with bourbon. Spread pecan frosting between layers. Spread top and sides of cake with chocolate frosting. For best flavor, cover and let stand at room temperature 8 to 24 hours before serving. Garnish, if desired. **Yield: 12 servings.**

Two-Part Frosting:

Split this frosting in half; add pecans to one part that becomes the filling, and cocoa to the rest that becomes the outer frosting.

Prep: 7 min.

1   cup butter, softened
2   (16-oz.) packages powdered sugar
½   cup milk
2   tsp. vanilla extract
1¼   cups chopped pecans, toasted
2   Tbsp. milk, divided
½   cup unsweetened cocoa

Beat butter at medium speed with an electric mixer until creamy. With mixer at low speed, gradually add 2 cups powdered sugar, beating until blended. Add ½ cup milk and vanilla, beating until blended.

Gradually add remaining powdered sugar, beating until smooth. Remove 3 cups frosting, and place in a separate bowl; stir in pecans and 1 Tbsp. milk. (This pecan frosting will be used as the filling.) Add cocoa and remaining 1 Tbsp. milk to frosting in mixing bowl, beating until blended. **Yield: 3 cups pecan frosting plus 1¾ cups chocolate frosting.**

Chocolate-Cherry Galettes

These individual freeform pastries are packed with plump cherries and chocolate chunks.

Prep: 27 min.   Cook: 22 min.   Other: 40 min.

4   cups all-purpose flour
1¼   cups granulated sugar, divided
2   tsp. salt
1½   cups butter, cut up and divided
1   cup ice water
1½   cups pecan halves, toasted
1   large egg
1½   cups semisweet chocolate chunks, divided
Parchment paper
2   (12-oz.) packages frozen dark, sweet cherries, thawed and well-drained
¼   tsp. almond extract
1   egg white
2   Tbsp. turbinado sugar

Whisk together flour, ½ cup sugar, and salt; cut in 1 cup butter with a pastry blender or fork until mixture resembles small peas and is crumbly. Sprinkle 1 cup ice water, ¼ cup at a time, over surface; stir with a fork until dry ingredients are moistened. Divide dough into 2 equal portions; wrap and chill.

While dough chills, process pecans and remaining ¾ cup sugar in a food processor 30 seconds. Add remaining ½ cup butter and 1 egg; process 1 minute or until smooth. Place 1 cup chocolate chunks in a microwave-safe bowl. Microwave at HIGH 1 minute or until melted; stir into pecan mixture. Cover and chill 30 minutes.

Preheat oven to 400°. Working with 1 portion at a time, roll dough to ⅛" thickness on a lightly floured surface. Cut 3 (8") circles from dough, and place each on a parchment paper-lined baking sheet. Spread ⅓ cup pecan filling over each dough circle, leaving a ½" border around edges.

Combine cherries and almond extract in a bowl. Spread ⅓ cup cherry mixture over each dough circle to within 2" of edges. Fold 1" borders of dough over cherries. Repeat with remaining dough, pecan filling, and cherries.

Whisk together egg white and 1 tablespoon water in a small bowl. Brush outer edges of galettes with egg wash; sprinkle with turbinado sugar.

Bake at 400° for 20 to 22 minutes or until golden. Sprinkle galettes with remaining ½ cup chocolate chunks. Let stand 10 minutes before serving. **Yield: 6 galettes.**

Chocolate Extreme Cupcakes

These triple chocolate cupcakes are a chocolate lover's dream.

Prep: 24 min.   Cook: 30 min.   Other: 50 min.

1   cup unsalted butter, softened
½   cup granulated sugar
1   cup firmly packed light brown sugar
4   large eggs
3   (1-oz.) unsweetened chocolate baking squares, melted
3   (1-oz.) semisweet chocolate baking squares, melted
1   tsp. vanilla extract
2   cups all-purpose flour
1   tsp. baking soda
½   tsp. salt
1   cup buttermilk
Jumbo paper baking cups
Thick Chocolate Frosting

Preheat oven to 350°. Beat butter at medium speed with an electric mixer until creamy. Gradually add sugars, beating well. Add eggs, 1 at a time, beating after each addition. Add melted chocolates and vanilla, beating well.

Combine flour, baking soda, and salt; add to batter alternately with buttermilk, beginning and ending with flour mixture. Beat at low speed after each addition until blended.

Place baking cups in jumbo muffin pans. Spoon batter into cups, filling three-fourths full.

Bake at 350° for 30 minutes or until a wooden pick inserted in center comes out clean. Cool in pans on wire racks 5 minutes. Remove from pans, and cool completely on wire racks (45 minutes). Spread with Thick Chocolate Frosting. **Yield: 1 dozen.**

Thick Chocolate Frosting:

Prep: 5 min.

½   cup butter, softened
1   (16-oz.) package powdered sugar
1   cup semisweet chocolate morsels, melted
½   cup whipping cream
2   tsp. vanilla extract
Pinch of salt

Beat butter at medium speed with an electric mixer until creamy; gradually add powdered sugar alternately with melted chocolate and whipping cream. Beat at low speed after each addition until blended. Stir in vanilla and salt. **Yield: 3½ cups.**

Chocolate Extreme Cupcakes

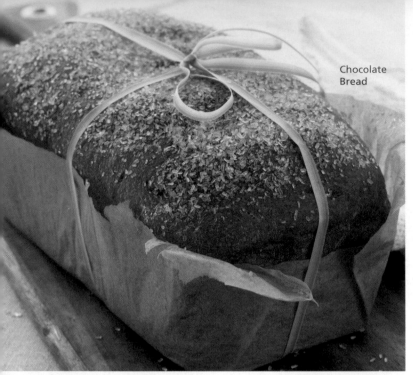

Chocolate
Bread

Combine milk, ½ cup warm water, and yeast in a large bowl; whisk until smooth. Let stand 5 minutes. Stir 2 cups flour, cocoa, granulated sugar, and salt into yeast mixture; beat at medium speed with an electric mixer until smooth. Beat in egg, butter, and 2 cups flour until a soft dough forms.

Turn out dough onto a floured surface, and knead until smooth (about 6 minutes), adding remaining ½ cup flour, 1 Tbsp. at a time as needed, to prevent dough from sticking. Fold in chopped chocolate during last minute of kneading.

Place dough in a large, lightly greased bowl, turning to coat top. Cover with plastic wrap, and let rise in a warm place (85°), free from drafts, 1 hour and 40 minutes or until doubled in bulk.

Punch down dough. Divide dough in half; gently shape each portion into an 8" x 4" oval. Place dough in 2 lightly greased 8½" x 4½" loaf pans. Cover and let rise 1½ hours or until doubled in bulk.

Preheat oven to 375°. Sprinkle loaves with turbinado sugar. Bake at 375° for 25 minutes or until loaves sound hollow when tapped. Remove from pans. Let cool on a wire rack. **Yield: 2 loaves.**

Fold/knead chopped chocolate into bread dough.

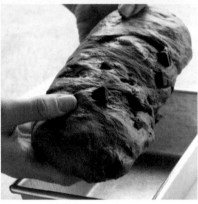

Place dough in loaf pans to rise.

Chocolate Bread

Save one of the loaves to turn into luscious Chocolate Bread Pudding (recipe at right), if you'd like.

Prep: 21 min.   Cook: 25 min.   Other: 3 hr., 15 min.

1¼   cups warm milk (100° to 110°)
½   cup warm water (100° to 110°)
1   (.25-oz.) package active dry yeast
4½   cups all-purpose flour, divided
½   cup unsweetened cocoa
¼   cup granulated sugar
1   tsp. salt
1   large egg
2   Tbsp. butter, softened
2   (4-oz.) semisweet chocolate bars, chopped
     (we tested with Ghirardelli)
1½   Tbsp. turbinado sugar

editor's favorite

Chocolate Bread Pudding

Prep: 16 min.   Cook: 1 hr., 6 min.   Other: 10 min.

2   cups milk
2   cups whipping cream
1   tsp. ground cinnamon
4   large eggs
1¼   cups sugar
2   Tbsp. butter, melted
1½   tsp. vanilla extract
1   loaf day-old Chocolate Bread (recipe at left),
     cut into 1" cubes
4   (1.4-oz) chocolate-coated toffee candy bars,
     chopped (we tested with SKOR)
1   cup semisweet chocolate morsels, divided

Preheat oven to 350°. Combine first 3 ingredients in a medium saucepan; cook over medium heat just until bubbles appear (do not boil). Whisk together eggs, sugar, and butter in a large bowl. Gradually add hot milk mixture to eggs, whisking constantly. Stir in vanilla.

Add bread cubes, chopped candy bars, and ½ cup chocolate morsels to milk mixture, stirring until bread is moistened. Pour into a lightly greased 13" x 9" baking dish.

Bake, covered, at 350° for 30 minutes. Uncover and bake 30 more minutes or until set. Remove from oven, and sprinkle with remaining ½ cup chocolate morsels. Let stand 10 minutes before serving. **Yield: 12 servings.**

editor's favorite • gift idea • make ahead
Chocolate Chunk Scones

Serve these big chocolate wedges for breakfast or brunch with coffee, or for dessert with a dollop of whipped cream.

Prep: 25 min.   Cook: 36 min.

4	cups all-purpose flour
⅔	cup sugar
½	cup unsweetened cocoa
4	tsp. baking powder
1½	tsp. baking soda
1	tsp. salt
½	tsp. freshly grated nutmeg
¾	cup cold butter, cut up
1	(11.5-ounce) package semisweet chocolate chunks
1	cup coarsely chopped walnuts or pecans (optional)
1¾	cups buttermilk
1	large egg, lightly beaten
2	tsp. vanilla extract

Parchment paper
2 Tbsp. sugar

Preheat oven to 350°. Whisk together flour and next 6 ingredients in a large bowl.

Cut butter into flour mixture with a pastry blender or fork until mixture resembles small peas and is crumbly. Stir in chocolate chunks and, if desired, nuts.

Combine buttermilk, egg, and vanilla. Pour over crumb mixture; stir just until dry ingredients are moistened.

Turn out dough onto a lightly floured surface, and gently knead 3 or 4 times.

Divide dough in half; shape each half into a ball. Pat each into a 6" circle on parchment paper-lined baking sheets. Cut each circle into 6 wedges using a sharp knife (do not separate wedges). Sprinkle 2 Tbsp. sugar over dough.

Bake at 350° for 36 minutes or until a wooden pick inserted in center comes out clean. Separate into wedges. Serve warm, or remove to a wire rack to cool. Reheat scones in microwave at HIGH 20 to 25 seconds each. **Yield: 1 dozen.**

Chocolate Bread Pudding

Chocolate Chunk Scones

Triple-Layer Peanut Butter Brownie Bars

Add eggs, 1 at a time, beating just until blended. Add vanilla. Add flour; beat at low speed just until blended. Stir in ¾ cup peanuts.

Spread batter into prepared pan.

Bake at 350° for 30 to 34 minutes. (Wooden pick will not test clean.) Remove to a wire rack, and cool completely.

Meanwhile, beat peanut butter and ½ cup butter in a large mixing bowl at medium speed until blended. Add powdered sugar; beat until blended. Spread over brownies.

Melt 8 oz. chocolate squares and remaining 1 oz. chopped chocolate in a small glass bowl according to microwave package directions; stir in corn syrup. Spoon dollops of melted chocolate over peanut butter layer; spread gently to cover peanut butter layer. Sprinkle with ⅓ cup peanuts, if desired. Cover and chill 2 hours or until set. Use foil to lift uncut brownies out of pan. Peel foil away from sides of uncut brownies, and cut into bars. **Yield: 2 dozen.**

editor's favorite • gift idea • make ahead
Triple-Layer Peanut Butter Brownie Bars

Prep: 17 min. Cook: 36 min. Other: 2 hr., 5 min.

1	cup butter
7	(1-oz.) semisweet chocolate baking squares, divided and chopped
2	cups granulated sugar
4	large eggs
1	tsp. vanilla extract
1	cup all-purpose flour
¾	cup dry-roasted peanuts, chopped
1	cup creamy peanut butter
½	cup butter, softened
1	cup powdered sugar
8	(1-oz.) semisweet chocolate baking squares
1	Tbsp. light corn syrup
⅓	cup dry-roasted peanuts, chopped (optional)

Preheat oven to 350°. Line a lightly greased 13" x 9" pan with aluminum foil, allowing foil to extend over ends of pan; set aside.

Melt 1 cup butter in a saucepan over medium heat. Remove from heat; add 6 oz. chopped chocolate, and let stand 5 minutes. Stir until smooth; transfer to a large mixing bowl.

Add 2 cups granulated sugar to melted chocolate mixture; beat at medium speed with an electric mixer until blended.

editor's favorite • make ahead • quick & easy
Ultimate Chocolate Pudding

Definitive in flavor and silky texture, this pudding deserves a place in the chocolate hall of fame.

Prep: 10 min. Cook: 12 min. Other: 10 min.

1¼	cups sugar
½	cup Dutch process cocoa
¼	cup cornstarch
½	tsp. salt
2½	cups milk
⅓	cup unsalted butter, cut up
2	tsp. vanilla extract

Unsweetened whipped cream
Chocolate-filled vanilla wafer sandwich cookies
    (we tested with Pepperidge Farm Milano cookies)

Whisk together first 4 ingredients in a medium saucepan. Gradually whisk in milk. Cook over medium heat, stirring constantly, until pudding boils and is thickened (about 8 to 10 minutes). Reduce heat to medium-low, and cook 2 more minutes. Remove from heat; add butter and vanilla, stirring gently until butter melts. Place heavy-duty plastic wrap directly on warm pudding (to keep a film from forming); cool 10 minutes.

Serve warm, or chill until ready to serve. Top with whipped cream. Serve with cookies. **Yield: 3½ cups.**

Note: For rich chocolate flavor, order double-Dutch dark cocoa online at www.kingarthurflour.com

Sweet-and-Spicy Glazed Turkey

TOP *Chicken & Turkey*

Turkey and chicken get top billing on the plate, as this mix of entrées promises great flavor, beautiful presentation, and lots of holiday flair.

Sweet-and-Spicy Glazed Turkey

Crushed red pepper kicks up the brown sugar-orange glaze that paints this turkey and gives it a slight Asian edge.

Prep: 12 min.   Cook: 2 hr., 48 min.   Other: 30 min.

1	cup orange juice
¼	cup firmly packed brown sugar
2	Tbsp. butter
1	tsp. crushed red pepper
1	tsp. orange zest
¼	tsp. salt
¼	tsp. freshly ground black pepper
1	(9- to 10-lb.) fresh or frozen turkey, thawed
1	orange, cut into 4 wedges
1	medium onion, cut into 4 wedges
2	Tbsp. butter, softened
1	tsp. salt
½	tsp. black pepper

Garnish: roasted Brussels sprouts

Combine first 7 ingredients in a medium saucepan; bring to a boil over medium-high heat. Reduce heat and simmer 15 minutes or until mixture is syrupy and reduced to about ⅔ cup. Set aside.

Preheat oven to 325°. Remove giblets and neck from turkey; discard or refrigerate for another use. Rinse turkey with cold water; pat dry with paper towels. Place turkey, breast side up, on a lightly greased rack in an aluminum foil-lined broiler pan. Lift wingtips up and over back, and tuck under bird.

Place orange and onion wedges inside turkey cavity. Rub softened butter all over outside of turkey, including legs. Tie ends of legs together with heavy string. Sprinkle turkey all over with 1 tsp. salt and ½ tsp. black pepper.

Bake, uncovered, at 325° for 1 hour. Brush turkey with half of the glaze; bake 1½ more hours or until a meat thermometer inserted into meaty part of thigh registers 170°, brushing with glaze every 30 minutes. Shield turkey with aluminum foil during cooking, if necessary, to prevent excessive browning.

Transfer turkey to a serving platter; cover turkey with foil, and let stand up to 30 minutes before carving. Garnish, if desired. **Yield: 9 to 10 servings.**

Note: Roast Brussels sprouts with a drizzle of olive oil on a rimmed baking sheet at 450° for 25 minutes or until browned.

Turkey Carving 101

To slice turkey easily, allow it to rest at room temperature after it's cooked, covered with aluminum foil, 15 minutes or more before carving. After the meal, remove leftover meat and stuffing from the carcass before storing in the refrigerator.

1. Carve the bird, breast side up, on a carving board in the kitchen or on a serving platter at the table.
2. Cut away string first. Remove stuffing to a serving bowl.
3. Grasp the end of a drumstick, and pull it away from the body. Cut through the skin and meat between the thigh and body; bend the leg away from the bird to expose the leg joint. Slice through the joint, and remove the leg. Cut through the joint that separates the thigh and drumstick. Slice the dark meat from the bones of the leg and thigh rather than placing them whole on the serving platter.
4. Cut the wings off at their second joint, leaving the upper part of the wing intact to steady the bird.
5. To carve the breast meat, steady the bird with a carving fork and make a deep horizontal cut into the breast just above the wing. (Use this cut to mark the end of each slice of breast meat.) Beginning at the outer top edge of breast, cut thin slices from the top down to the horizontal cut. Carve from one side of the turkey at a time, carving only as much meat as needed for serving.

Roasted Lemon Chicken

Try your own combination of herbs in this simple entrée.
Regular basting gives the finished bird crispy brown skin.

Prep: 25 min.   Cook: 1 hr., 16 min.   Other: 15 min.

1½   lemons
2   large garlic cloves, minced
2   Tbsp. unsalted butter, softened and divided
2   Tbsp. minced fresh oregano, divided
2   Tbsp. minced fresh thyme, divided
1   tsp. salt, divided
½   tsp. pepper, divided
1   (4-lb.) whole chicken
2   Tbsp. minced fresh flat-leaf parsley

Preheat oven to 400°. Grate zest from 1 lemon to equal 2 tsp. Pierce zested lemon several times with a paring knife. Squeeze juice from remaining lemon half into a measuring cup to equal 1 Tbsp. Set lemon juice aside.

Combine zest; garlic; 1 Tbsp. each of butter, oregano, and thyme; ½ tsp. salt, and ¼ tsp. pepper in a small bowl, stirring until blended. Loosen and lift skin from chicken with fingers, without totally detaching skin; spread half of butter mixture underneath. Carefully replace skin. Sprinkle remaining 1 Tbsp. herbs, remaining ½ tsp. salt, and remaining ¼ tsp. pepper inside cavity; rub into cavity. Spread remaining half of butter mixture on skin; rub into skin. Place zested lemon in cavity. Tie ends of legs together with string; tuck wingtips under. Place chicken on a lightly greased wire rack in a lightly greased roasting pan.

Bake at 400° for 1 hour and 15 minutes or until a thermometer inserted in thickest portion of thigh registers 170°, basting with drippings every 20 minutes. Transfer chicken to a plate; transfer drippings to a small saucepan. Cover chicken with aluminum foil, and let stand 15 minutes before carving.

Bring drippings to a boil. Add remaining 1 Tbsp. butter to pan, stirring until melted. Remove from heat, and stir in accumulated juices from chicken, reserved lemon juice, and parsley. Carve chicken, and place on a serving platter; drizzle sauce over chicken. **Yield: 4 servings.**

---

editor's favorite

Herb-Roasted Turkey Breast With Harvest Vegetables

Succulent turkey breast is surrounded by vibrant roasted fall vegetables, savory bacon, and toasted pecans.

Prep: 31 min.   Cook: 2 hr., 10 min.   Other: 15 min.

1   Tbsp. chopped fresh rosemary
1   Tbsp. chopped fresh thyme
4   garlic cloves, minced
1   tsp. salt
½   tsp. pepper, divided
1   (6- to 7-lb.) bone-in turkey breast
1   Tbsp. olive oil
1   (3-lb.) butternut squash, cut into 1½" pieces
1½   lb. turnips, peeled and cut into 1½" pieces
4   medium carrots, cut into 1½" pieces
1   large onion, cut into 1½" pieces
2   Tbsp. olive oil
½   tsp. salt
⅛   tsp. pepper
4   thick bacon slices
½   cup coarsely chopped pecans
2   tsp. chopped fresh rosemary
½   tsp. salt
2½   to 2¾ cups chicken broth
3   Tbsp. all-purpose flour
Garnish: fresh rosemary sprigs

Preheat oven to 400°. Stir together first 4 ingredients and ¼ tsp. pepper in a small bowl. Starting at neck cavity, loosen and lift skin from turkey breast with fingers, without totally detaching skin. Rub herb mixture under skin; carefully replace skin. Rub 1 Tbsp. oil over outside of turkey. Place turkey, breast side up, on a lightly greased rack in a lightly greased large roasting pan. Bake at 400° for 1 hour and 15 minutes.

Meanwhile, combine squash and next 6 ingredients in a large bowl. Arrange one-third of vegetables around turkey in pan. Place remaining vegetables in another lightly greased roasting pan. Continue cooking turkey and vegetables 45 more minutes or until vegetables are tender and a meat thermometer inserted into thickest part of turkey breast registers 170°. Transfer vegetables to a bowl using a slotted spoon, reserving drippings in pan. Cover turkey with foil, and let stand 15 minutes before slicing.

While turkey stands, cook bacon in a skillet until crisp; remove bacon, reserving drippings in skillet. Crumble

Herb-Roasted Turkey Breast With
Harvest Vegetables

bacon; set aside. Sauté pecans in hot drippings in skillet 2 to 3 minutes or until pecans are toasted. Remove pecans from skillet using a slotted spoon. Add pecans, reserved bacon, 2 tsp. rosemary, and ½ tsp. salt to vegetables; toss to combine.

To make gravy, pour pan drippings into a 4-cup glass measuring cup, and let stand 5 minutes. Spoon 2 Tbsp. fat out of drippings in cup and return to roasting pan; discard remaining fat. Add enough chicken broth to measuring cup to yield 3 cups. Set aside.

Place roasting pan over 2 burners on the stovetop over medium heat. Gradually whisk in flour, and cook, whisking constantly, 2 minutes or until flour is lightly browned. Add reserved broth to pan; stir until browned bits are loosened from bottom of pan. Bring to a boil; reduce heat, and simmer 8 minutes or until gravy is reduced to 2½ cups. Stir in remaining ¼ tsp. pepper. Serve gravy with turkey and roasted vegetables. Garnish, if desired. **Yield: 10 to 12 servings.**

Turkey Panini

Try a trendy sandwich using leftover turkey after the big holiday feast. Pile on the turkey and use your homemade cranberry sauce, if desired. Shaved deli turkey is a fine substitute.

Prep: 10 min.   Cook: 3 min.

¼   cup whole-berry cranberry sauce
2   to 3 tsp. prepared horseradish
2   Tbsp. mayonnaise
4   large slices ciabatta bread (½" thick)
4   (⅜"-thick) slices cooked turkey breast
     or deli turkey
Salt and pepper to taste
4   (¾-oz.) provolone cheese slices
4   bacon slices, cooked
1½   Tbsp. olive oil
Garnish: gourmet mixed salad greens

   Preheat panini press according to manufacturer's instructions. Combine cranberry sauce and horseradish, stirring well.
   Spread mayonnaise on 1 side of each slice of bread. Spread cranberry-horseradish sauce on 2 slices of bread; top each sandwich with 2 turkey slices, and sprinkle with salt and pepper.
   Arrange 2 cheese slices on each sandwich; top with 2 bacon slices. Cover with tops of bread, mayonnaise side down.

   Brush tops of sandwiches with olive oil. Turn and brush bottoms of sandwiches with olive oil.
   Place sandwiches in a panini press; cook 3 minutes or until cheese begins to melt and bread is toasted. Serve hot. Garnish, if desired. **Yield: 2 sandwiches.**

Crispy Chicken Salad With Dried Cranberries, Walnuts, and Blue Cheese

Panko breadcrumbs are the key to the crispy chicken strips featured in this colorful salad.

Prep: 23 min.   Cook: 17 min.

¼   cup red wine vinegar
1   Tbsp. Dijon mustard
½   tsp. salt
¼   tsp. pepper
½   cup extra virgin olive oil
8   cups gourmet mixed salad greens
1   cup diced cucumber
6   green onions, sliced
⅔   cup dried cranberries
½   cup crumbled blue cheese
5   chicken cutlets (about 1 pound)
½   tsp. salt
½   tsp. pepper
1   large egg, lightly beaten
1   cup Japanese breadcrumbs (panko)
1   cup vegetable oil
1   cup walnut halves, coarsely chopped and toasted

   Whisk together first 4 ingredients in a small bowl. Add olive oil in a slow, steady stream, whisking constantly until smooth.
   Combine salad greens and next 4 ingredients in a large bowl. Cover and chill while preparing chicken.
   Sprinkle chicken with ½ teaspoon each salt and pepper. Dip chicken in egg; dredge in breadcrumbs.
   Fry chicken cutlets, in 2 batches, in hot vegetable oil in a large skillet over medium-high heat 2 to 3 minutes on each side or until golden and crisp. Drain on paper towels. Cut each cutlet crosswise into ½" slices.
   Toss salad with ⅓ cup dressing; add walnuts, and toss gently. Divide salad among 4 serving plates; top each serving with sliced chicken, and drizzle with desired amount of dressing. **Yield: 4 servings.**

Turkey Panini

Crispy Chicken Salad With Dried Cranberries, Walnuts, and Blue Cheese

Turkey Breast Roulades With Collards and Bacon

Collards and bacon—two Southern greats—are showcased in this rolled entrée. Find packaged, chopped collard greens in the produce department of grocery stores.

Prep: 16 min.   Cook: 1 hr., 3 min.   Other: 10 min.

6	bacon slices
1	small onion, chopped
2	garlic cloves, minced
2¼	cups chicken broth, divided
4	cups firmly packed chopped collard greens
¼	cup fine, dry breadcrumbs
½	tsp. salt, divided
½	tsp. hot sauce, divided
1	(3-lb.) boneless turkey breast
½	tsp. freshly ground pepper
1	Tbsp. all-purpose flour
1	Tbsp. whipping cream

Cook bacon in a large skillet over medium heat 4 minutes just until fat is rendered. Remove 4 partially cooked bacon slices, and set aside. Cook remaining 2 bacon slices 5 minutes or until crisp. Remove bacon from skillet, and drain on paper towels, reserving drippings in pan. Crumble bacon, and set aside.

Sauté onion in hot drippings 3 minutes. Add garlic, and sauté 1 more minute. Add 1½ cups broth and collard greens to pan; cover and bring to a boil. Cook 18 minutes or until tender. Uncover and cook, stirring often, 3 to 4 minutes or until most of broth evaporates. Remove from heat, and stir in breadcrumbs, ¼ tsp. salt, and ¼ tsp. hot sauce.

Preheat oven to 400°. Butterfly turkey by making a lengthwise cut in 1 side, cutting to but not through the opposite side; unfold. Place between 2 sheets of heavy-duty plastic wrap, and flatten to ½" thickness, using a rolling pin or the flat side of a meat mallet. Sprinkle both sides of turkey with remaining ¼ tsp. each salt and pepper. Spoon greens mixture over turkey, leaving a 2" border. Roll up, starting at 1 long side. Arrange 4 reserved bacon slices in a crisscross pattern over turkey; tie with kitchen string, securing at 2" intervals. Place, seam side down, in a lightly greased jelly-roll pan.

Bake at 400° for 40 to 42 minutes or until a meat thermometer inserted into thickest portion registers 170°. Remove from oven; let stand 10 minutes before slicing.

For sauce, transfer drippings into a glass measuring cup, scraping pan to remove browned bits. Add enough remaining broth, about ¾ cup, to equal 1 cup. Pour into a medium saucepan; add flour, and whisk until smooth. Bring to a boil over medium-high heat, whisking constantly. Cook 3 minutes or until thickened. Whisk in cream and remaining ¼ tsp. hot sauce. Stir in reserved crumbled bacon. **Yield: 6 to 8 servings.**

Chicken Cobbler With Cream
Cheese Crust

Chicken Cobbler With Cream Cheese Crust

This old-fashioned comfort dish includes succulent chunks of chicken and saucy garden vegetables, all topped with a flaky cream cheese pastry.

Prep: 46 min.   Cook: 2 hr., 27 min.   Other: 45 min.

1	(3½-lb.) whole chicken
1½	tsp. salt, divided
	Cream Cheese Crust
	Parchment paper
8	oz. fresh green beans, trimmed and cut into 1" pieces (about 1½ cups)
6	Tbsp. butter, divided
1⅓	cups sliced fresh mushrooms
2	carrots, cut in half lengthwise and sliced
1	medium onion, chopped
1	celery rib, sliced
2	garlic cloves, minced
½	cup all-purpose flour
½	cup heavy whipping cream
2	tsp. chopped fresh sage
¼	tsp. pepper
1	large egg, lightly beaten

Rinse chicken, and pat dry; remove excess fat. Place chicken, giblets, ¾ tsp. salt, and 3½ cups water in a Dutch oven. Bring to a boil over medium-high heat; reduce heat to low. Cover and simmer 1 hour and 15 minutes or until chicken is done. Remove from heat. Remove chicken from broth; let cool 30 minutes. Strain broth to measure 3 cups, reserving giblets for another use.

While chicken cools, prepare dough for Cream Cheese Crust; shape dough into a 1"-thick disk. Place disk on a large piece of parchment paper.

Lightly grease a 2-qt. oval baking dish. Roll out dough on parchment until it is ½" larger than diameter of baking dish. Transfer dough and paper to a large baking sheet. Chill 30 minutes to 24 hours.

Skin and bone chicken; chop meat into bite-size pieces to measure 4 cups. Cook green beans in boiling water to cover in a saucepan 8 minutes or until tender. Drain and set aside.

Melt 2 Tbsp. butter in a large skillet over medium-high heat; add mushrooms, next 4 ingredients, and ¼ teaspoon salt. Cook, stirring often, 8 minutes or until vegetables are tender. Remove pan from heat.

Preheat oven to 400°. Melt remaining ¼ cup butter in a heavy saucepan over low heat; whisk in flour until smooth. Cook, whisking constantly, 1 minute. Gradually whisk in reserved broth; cook over medium heat, whisking constantly, 5 minutes or until thickened and bubbly. Stir in remaining ½ tsp. salt, cream, sage, and pepper. Pour sauce over vegetables in skillet. Add chicken and green beans, stirring until coated with sauce. Pour filling into prepared dish.

Remove pastry from refrigerator. Remove parchment from top of pastry. Cut leaves or decorative shapes in pastry using a cookie cutter. Let pastry stand 3 to 5 minutes or until pliable.

Cover filling with pastry, pressing edges of dough to sides of dish; brush pastry with beaten egg.

Bake at 400° for 35 minutes or until crust is golden and filling is bubbly. Let stand 10 minutes before serving. **Yield: 6 servings.**

Note: For ease in transferring pastry, carefully roll dough onto a rolling pin, and then unroll onto filling.

make ahead

Cream Cheese Crust:

Prep: 5 min.   Other: 30 min.

1¼	cups all-purpose flour
4	oz. cold cream cheese
¼	cup cold butter, cut into 4 pieces
¼	tsp. salt

Process all ingredients in a food processor 1 minute or until dough forms a ball and leaves sides of bowl. Roll out dough as recipe directs. **Yield: enough pastry for 1 cobbler.**

Bay-Scented Roast Turkey

Cutting up a turkey is just like cutting up a chicken for frying; it's just a bigger bird.

Prep: 30 min.   Cook: 1 hr., 26 min.   Other: 15 min.

11	garlic cloves, divided
2	carrots, cut into 1" pieces
3	celery ribs, cut into 2" pieces
2	onions, cut into 2" pieces
4	fresh thyme sprigs
1	(32-oz.) container chicken broth
¼	cup butter, cut into 4 pieces
½	tsp. salt
1¼	tsp. freshly ground pepper, divided
1	(14-lb.) turkey, cut up
12	fresh bay leaves
⅓	cup all-purpose flour
¼	cup dry white wine

Preheat oven to 375°. Place 3 garlic cloves and next 4 ingredients in a large roasting pan. Pour broth over vegetables.

With processor running, drop remaining 8 garlic cloves through food chute; process until minced. Add butter, salt, and 1 tsp. pepper through food chute; process until combined. Reserve back, wings, neck, and giblets from turkey for another use. Loosen and lift skin from turkey breast and leg quarters with fingers, without totally detaching skin; spread half of butter mixture under skin. Place 2 to 3 bay leaves under skin of each piece of turkey; carefully replace skin. Rub skin with remaining half of butter mixture. Place turkey leg quarters on top of vegetables.

Bake at 375° for 10 minutes; add breasts, and bake 25 more minutes. Increase oven temperature to 425°; bake 40 minutes or until a meat thermometer inserted into thickest part of breast registers 170°.

Transfer turkey to a platter; cover loosely with aluminum foil, and let stand 15 minutes. Strain broth through a wire-mesh strainer, discarding vegetables.

Pour 4 cups broth into a medium saucepan, reserving remaining broth for another use. Bring broth to a boil over medium-high heat. Stir together flour, wine, and remaining ¼ tsp. pepper; add to broth, and cook over medium-high heat, stirring constantly, 8 minutes or until thickened. Serve gravy with turkey. **Yield: 10 servings.**

---

editor's favorite

Party Paella Casserole

Here's a great use for rotisserie chicken, shrimp, and yellow rice.

Prep: 26 min.   Cook: 43 min.   Other: 30 min.

2	(8-oz.) packages yellow rice (we tested with Vigo)
1	lb. medium peeled shrimp
1	Tbsp. fresh lemon juice (about ½ large lemon)
½	tsp. salt
¼	tsp. pepper
2	large garlic cloves, minced
1½	Tbsp. olive oil
1	(2½-lb.) lemon-and-garlic deli-roasted whole chicken, coarsely shredded
5	large green onions, chopped (about 1 cup)
1	(8-oz.) container sour cream
1	cup frozen English peas, thawed
1	cup pimiento-stuffed Spanish olives, coarsely chopped
1½	cups (6 oz.) shredded Monterey Jack cheese
½	tsp. smoked Spanish paprika

Prepare rice according to package directions. Remove from heat, and let cool 30 minutes; fluff with a fork.

Meanwhile, toss shrimp with lemon juice, salt, and pepper in a bowl. Sauté seasoned shrimp and garlic in hot oil in a large nonstick skillet 2 minutes or just until done. Remove from heat.

Preheat oven to 400°. Combine shredded chicken, rice, green onions, sour cream, and peas in a large bowl; toss well. Add shrimp and olives, tossing gently. Spoon rice mixture into a greased 13" x 9" baking dish.

Combine cheese and paprika, tossing well; sprinkle over casserole.

Bake, uncovered, at 400° for 15 minutes or just until cheese is melted and casserole is thoroughly heated. **Yield: 8 servings.**

Party Paella Casserole

Mediterranean Chicken Kebabs

Donned with bell pepper, red onion wedges, and herbs, these tasty skewers are sure to please all year long.

Prep: 18 min.   Cook: 10 min.   Other: 30 min.

3	large garlic cloves, crushed
2	Tbsp. minced fresh rosemary
1	Tbsp. minced fresh oregano
1	tsp. salt, divided
½	tsp. pepper, divided
¼	cup fresh lemon juice, divided
6	Tbsp. olive oil, divided
1½	lbs. boned and skinned chicken breasts, cut into 1" pieces
1	large red bell pepper, cut into 1" pieces
1	large red onion, cut into 1" wedges
6	(10" to 12") metal skewers

Combine first 3 ingredients, ½ tsp. salt, ¼ tsp. pepper, 3 Tbsp. lemon juice, and 5 Tbsp. oil in a large shallow dish or zip-top plastic freezer bag; add chicken, turning to coat. Cover or seal, and chill 30 minutes. Combine remaining ½ tsp. salt, ¼ tsp. pepper, 1 Tbsp. lemon juice, and 1 Tbsp. oil in a small bowl; set aside.

Preheat grill. Thread marinated chicken, bell pepper, and onion alternately onto skewers, discarding marinade. Grill over medium-high heat (350° to 400°) for 8 to 10 minutes or until done, turning occasionally and basting with reserved olive oil mixture. **Yield: 6 servings.**

---

editor's favorite

Chile-Rubbed Turkey Breast With Fresh Cranberry-Candied Pecan Salsa

The holiday bird goes south of the border in this spicy recipe. We especially liked the candied pecans in the salsa.

Prep: 30 min.   Cook: 2 hr., 23 min.   Other: 15 min.

2	ancho chile peppers, seeded and torn into pieces
4	garlic cloves
2	Tbsp. olive oil, divided
1	tsp. sugar
1	tsp. ground cumin
1	tsp. fresh lime juice
1	tsp. salt
1	(6- to 7-lb.) bone-in turkey breast

Fresh Cranberry-Candied Pecan Salsa
Garnish: fresh cilantro sprig

Combine ¾ cup water, chiles, and garlic in a small saucepan. Bring to a boil; reduce heat, and simmer, uncovered, 10 to 12 minutes or until most of liquid evaporates.

Process chile mixture, 1 Tbsp. oil, and next 4 ingredients in a food processor 1½ to 2 minutes or until smooth.

Preheat oven to 400°. Loosen and lift skin from turkey with fingers, without totally detaching skin; spread chile mixture under skin. Carefully replace skin. Rub skin with remaining 1 Tbsp. oil. Place breast on a lightly greased wire rack in a roasting pan.

Bake at 400° for 2 hours or until a meat thermometer inserted into thickest part of breast registers 170°. (Loosely cover with aluminum foil during baking, if needed, to prevent excessive browning.) Cover breast with aluminum foil, and let stand 15 minutes before carving. Serve with Fresh Cranberry-Candied Pecan Salsa. Garnish, if desired. **Yield: 8 to 10 servings.**

---

editor's favorite • make ahead • quick & easy

Fresh Cranberry-Candied Pecan Salsa:

Prep: 15 min.   Cook: 12 min.

	Parchment paper
¼	cup sugar
½	cup chopped pecans, toasted
1	(12-oz.) package fresh or frozen cranberries, partially thawed
⅓	cup honey
¼	cup thinly sliced green onions
1	tsp. lime zest
2	Tbsp. fresh lime juice
1	jalapeño pepper, seeded and minced (1½ Tbsp.)
¼	cup chopped fresh cilantro

Place a piece of parchment paper on work surface.

Cook sugar in a medium skillet over medium heat 3 minutes or until melted. Stir in pecans until coated. Pour candied pecans onto parchment paper, and cool completely; chop into small pieces.

Pulse cranberries and next 5 ingredients in a food processor 10 to 12 times or until chopped. Transfer to a bowl. Cover and chill until ready to serve. Stir in pecans and cilantro just before serving. **Yield: 3 cups.**

Chile-Rubbed Turkey Breast
With Fresh Cranberry-Candied
Pecan Salsa

Succotash With Smoked Ham and Herbs

CHOOSING *Sides*

Side dishes take center stage with these recipes that highlight winter's best ingredients and easy cooking methods.

editor's favorite

Succotash With Smoked Ham and Herbs

Fresh tarragon adds a subtle and intriguing flavor note to this rich, colorful side that's suitable with ham or pork roast.

Prep: 12 min.   Cook: 36 min.

1	(1-lb.) package frozen baby lima beans, thawed
2	Tbsp. unsalted butter
6	oz. smoked ham, coarsely chopped (about 1½ cups)
½	cup chopped red bell pepper
⅓	cup minced shallots
1	(1-lb.) package frozen baby gold and white corn, thawed (we tested with Birds Eye)
2	tsp. sugar
½	tsp. salt
½	tsp. freshly ground black pepper
1	cup heavy whipping cream
1	Tbsp. minced fresh chives
1	Tbsp. minced fresh parsley
1	Tbsp. minced fresh tarragon

Cook lima beans according to microwave package directions. Drain.

Melt butter in a large skillet over medium-high heat. Add ham; sauté 3 minutes or until lightly browned. Add red bell pepper and shallots; sauté 3 minutes or just until tender. Add lima beans, corn, and next 3 ingredients; cook, stirring often, 6 minutes. Add cream; cook, stirring often, 10 minutes or until vegetables are tender and cream is slightly thickened. Stir in herbs. **Yield: 6 to 8 servings.**

editor's favorite

Tangy Cauliflower With Tomatoes, Olives, and Feta

With a great blend of Mediterranean flavors, the highlight of this big-yield side dish is pockets of warm feta.

Prep: 6 min.   Cook: 31 min.

1	large head cauliflower (about 2 lb.), cut into florets
2	Tbsp. extra virgin olive oil
1	small red onion, thinly sliced
⅛	tsp. salt
¼	tsp. freshly ground pepper
1	(8-oz.) package feta cheese, cut into ½" cubes
2	Tbsp. white wine vinegar
2	tsp. sugar
2	plum tomatoes, chopped
1	cup pitted kalamata olives, coarsely chopped

Garnish: chopped fresh oregano

Bring 4 qt. salted water to a boil in a large Dutch oven over high heat. Add cauliflower; cook, stirring often, just until crisp-tender. Drain; rinse under cold water. Let cool in colander.

Heat oil in a large skillet or sauté pan over medium-high heat; add onion, salt, and pepper, and sauté 8 minutes or until onion is browned. Add cauliflower, cheese, and next 3 ingredients. Cook, stirring often, 3 minutes or until thoroughly heated. Sprinkle with olives. Garnish, if desired. **Yield: 8 servings.**

Heat a large, deep skillet over medium-high heat. Add oil and next 3 ingredients, stirring well with a whisk. Cook, whisking constantly, 1 to 2 minutes or until mixture is thickened. Stir in carrots, green onions, and desired amount of salt and pepper. Cook 1 to 2 minutes or until thoroughly heated. **Yield: 6 to 8 servings.**

editor's favorite

Braised Fennel and Leeks

Thinly sliced fennel and leeks simmer in a white wine broth and get an herbed crumb topping. Match this side with a pork roast, chicken, or fish.

Prep: 20 min.   Cook: 1 hr., 30 min.   Other: 10 min.

3	medium fennel bulbs
5	medium leeks, white and light green parts only, halved lengthwise and thinly sliced
1	(14-oz.) can chicken broth
⅓	cup dry white wine
2	Tbsp. chopped fresh parsley
1	tsp. chopped fresh thyme
¾	tsp. salt
¾	tsp. pepper
¼	cup butter, cut into pieces

Heavy-duty aluminum foil

2	cups fresh breadcrumbs
¼	cup olive oil
2	Tbsp. chopped fresh thyme

Preheat oven to 400°. Rinse fennel thoroughly. Trim and discard root ends of fennel bulbs. Trim stalks from bulbs, reserving fronds for another use. Cut bulbs into thin slices. Arrange fennel and leeks in a lightly greased 13" x 9" baking dish.

Combine chicken broth and next 5 ingredients, and pour over vegetables. Dot with butter, and cover tightly with heavy-duty aluminum foil. Bake at 400° for 1 hour.

Meanwhile, combine breadcrumbs, olive oil, and 2 Tbsp. thyme. Sprinkle breadcrumb mixture over vegetables. Bake, uncovered, 30 more minutes or until breadcrumbs are browned and liquid almost evaporates. Let stand 10 minutes before serving. **Yield: 10 servings.**

Braised Fennel and Leeks

Mustardy Carrots With Lemon and Green Onions

Serve these glazed carrots with lemon wedges to squeeze over the top for a citrus splash.

Prep: 12 min.   Cook: 25 min.

2	lb. carrots, peeled and coarsely chopped
2	Tbsp. olive oil
1	Tbsp. lemon juice
1	Tbsp. Dijon mustard
1	Tbsp. honey
¾	cup thinly sliced green onions

Salt and pepper to taste

Cook carrots in boiling salted water to cover 13 to 15 minutes or until tender; drain.

Sautéed Mushrooms With Sage and Pistachios

Using a combination of mushrooms adds layers of flavor. Cooking them without stirring browns them nicely.

Prep: 3 min.   Cook: 17 min.

2   Tbsp. olive oil
1½   lb. assorted mushrooms, quartered or sliced
        (we tested with shiitake, baby bella, and fresh
        button mushrooms)
3   Tbsp. butter
1   small onion, chopped
1   Tbsp. sherry vinegar or red wine vinegar
½   tsp. salt
⅛   tsp. pepper
⅓   cup heavy whipping cream
1½   Tbsp. chopped fresh sage
¼   cup roasted and salted pistachio nuts, coarsely
        chopped

Heat oil in a large skillet over medium-high heat. Add mushrooms; cook 10 minutes (do not stir). Add butter; stir until butter melts. Add onion and next 3 ingredients; cook, stirring occasionally, 4 minutes or until onion is tender. Reduce heat to medium; add cream and sage, stirring well. Cook, stirring constantly, 1 minute or until cream thickens.

Transfer mushrooms to a serving bowl; sprinkle with pistachios. **Yield: 4 to 6 servings.**

editor's favorite

Roasted Beets and Oranges With Herb Butter

These beets get a citrus infusion from roasting in a foil pack along with orange slices.

Prep: 15 min.   Cook: 1 hr., 29 min.

4   medium beets, trimmed, peeled, and cut into
        1" pieces (about 1 lb.)
1   small orange, halved lengthwise and thinly sliced
2   Tbsp. olive oil
¼   tsp. salt
¼   tsp. freshly ground pepper
3   Tbsp. butter, softened
1   Tbsp. chopped fresh flat-leaf parsley
1   Tbsp. chopped fresh rosemary
2   Tbsp. orange juice

Preheat oven to 400°. Combine first 5 ingredients in a large bowl; toss to coat. Wrap beets and oranges in lightly greased aluminum foil. Fold foil to seal. Transfer foil pack to a baking sheet.

Roast at 400° for 45 minutes. Carefully unfold foil with tongs, and continue roasting 40 more minutes or until beets are tender and browned. Remove beets and oranges from foil.

Melt butter in a large skillet over medium-high heat; whisk in herbs and orange juice, and cook 1 to 2 minutes or until slightly thickened. Add beets and oranges; sauté 1 to 2 minutes or until thoroughly heated. Transfer to a serving bowl. **Yield: 4 servings.**

editor's favorite

Caramelized Turnips

If you don't like turnips, this recipe may just change your mind. If you can only get baby turnips, cook them whole, and add 2 to 3 minutes to the cook time.

Prep: 8 min.   Cook: 40 min.

2   lb. turnips, peeled and cut into 1" pieces
        (about 5 cups)
2   Tbsp. unsalted butter
1½   Tbsp. sugar
½   tsp. salt
¼   tsp. freshly ground pepper

Place turnips in a single layer in a large skillet. Add enough water to cover two-thirds of turnips (to a depth of about ½"). Add butter and remaining ingredients. Bring to a boil; cover, reduce heat, and simmer 5 minutes. Uncover; cook over medium-high heat 30 to 32 minutes or until water evaporates and turnips are browned. Add 2 Tbsp. water; cook 1 minute to deglaze skillet, stirring to loosen particles from bottom of skillet and glaze turnips. Serve hot. **Yield: 4 to 6 servings.**

Whole Acorn Squash
Cream Soup

Whole Acorn Squash Cream Soup

This unique recipe celebrates the beauty of squash by using it as a serving vessel. Choose squash that stand upright for ease in baking and serving.

Prep: 16 min.   Cook: 1 hr., 45 min.

4	medium acorn squash
¼	cup cream cheese
1	cup heavy whipping cream
1	cup chicken broth
½	tsp. salt
1	tsp. ground cinnamon

Preheat oven to 350°. Cut off about 1" of stem ends of squash to reveal seeds. Scoop out and discard seeds and membranes. Arrange squash in a 13" x 9" baking dish.

Place 1 Tbsp. cream cheese in each squash cavity. Pour ¼ cup each heavy cream and chicken broth over cream cheese in each squash, and sprinkle each cavity with ⅛ tsp. salt and ¼ tsp. cinnamon. Add water to baking dish to a depth of ½".

Bake squash, uncovered, at 350° for 1 hour and 45 minutes or until squash are very tender.

To serve, carefully set each squash in a shallow soup bowl. **Yield: 4 servings.**

Roasted Tomatoes Provençale

An herb-and-garlic crumb topping dresses up fresh tomatoes for an easy accompaniment to meat, poultry, or fish.

Prep: 17 min.   Cook: 30 min.

4	medium-size firm ripe tomatoes (about 2 lb.), cut in half crosswise
¼	cup extra virgin olive oil, divided
3	large garlic cloves, thinly sliced
1	Tbsp. minced fresh thyme
¾	tsp. salt
¼	tsp. pepper
⅔	cup fresh breadcrumbs
3	Tbsp. minced fresh flat-leaf parsley

Preheat oven to 425°. Place tomato halves in a shallow baking dish. Drizzle 2 Tbsp. oil over tomatoes; sprinkle with garlic slices, thyme, salt, and pepper.

Roast at 425° for 20 minutes or until tomato juices are bubbly and tomatoes are just tender.

Combine breadcrumbs, parsley, and remaining 2 Tbsp. oil in a small bowl. Sprinkle crumb mixture over tomatoes. Bake 10 more minutes or until crumbs are browned. **Yield: 4 servings.**

Note: Make fresh breadcrumbs from your favorite crusty bread. Tear off or cut 1 or 2 thick slices, and pulse in a mini chopper or food processor until coarse crumbs form.

quick & easy

Asparagus With Gremolata

Gremolata is a parsley-lemon garnish typically sprinkled over Osso Bucco. Here it makes a nice adornment to fresh asparagus. We also recommend gremolata on baked potatoes and grilled chicken.

Prep: 4 min.   Cook: 13 min.

1	lemon
¼	cup chopped fresh flat-leaf parsley
2	garlic cloves, chopped
1	lb. fresh asparagus
2	Tbsp. unsalted butter, melted
½	tsp. salt
¼	tsp. pepper

Grate enough zest from lemon to yield about 2 tsp. Process parsley and garlic in a food processor until finely minced; add lemon zest, and set gremolata aside.

Snap off and discard tough ends of asparagus. Cook asparagus in boiling salted water to cover 5 to 6 minutes or until crisp-tender; drain. Arrange asparagus on a platter. Drizzle with butter; sprinkle with salt and pepper. Sprinkle with gremolata. **Yield: 4 servings.**

Chipotle Green Beans With Bacon

Look for canned chipotle peppers in adobo sauce in the Mexican-foods section of your grocery store.

Prep: 15 min.   Cook: 28 min.

8   bacon slices, chopped
½   medium onion, chopped (about 1¼ cups)
½   cup chicken broth
1   tsp. chopped canned chipotle peppers in
     adobo sauce
2   tsp. adobo sauce from can
¼   tsp. salt
¼   tsp. freshly ground black pepper
2   lb. fresh green beans, trimmed

Heat a large skillet over medium heat; add bacon, and cook 8 to 9 minutes or until browned and crisp. Drain bacon on paper towels, reserving 2 Tbsp. drippings in skillet. Sauté onion in hot drippings 4 to 5 minutes or until browned. Stir in broth and next 4 ingredients. Add green beans; toss to coat. Cover and cook 14 minutes or until tender, stirring often. Transfer beans to a serving dish; top with bacon. **Yield: 6 servings.**

Fix It Faster: Use 2 (12-oz.) packages pre-trimmed green beans.

Asparagus With Gremolata

Chipotle Green Beans With Bacon

FILL THE HEARTS OF FRIENDS AND FAMILY WITH THE SPIRIT OF THE SEASON
WHEN YOU PRESENT THEM WITH DELECTABLE TREATS FROM THE KITCHEN AND
GIFTS YOU MAKE YOURSELF.

Giving

Easy Chocolate Chip Cookie
Fudge

SWEET *Gifts*

Keep everyone on your gift list happy this holiday season with fifteen sweet ideas from the kitchen.

editor's favorite • gift idea • make ahead

Easy Chocolate Chip Cookie Fudge

This simple fudge requires little work but yields spectacular results.

Prep: 10 min.   Cook: 5 min.   Other: 4 hr.

1	(12-oz.) package semisweet chocolate morsels
1	(11.5-oz.) package milk chocolate morsels
½	cup evaporated milk
1	cup chopped pecans, toasted
1½	tsp. vanilla extract
¼	tsp. salt
1¾	cups coarsely chopped chocolate chip cookies (we tested with 12 Chips Ahoy cookies)

Line a lightly greased 8" square baking dish with aluminum foil. Set aside.

Combine first 3 ingredients in a medium saucepan; cook, stirring constantly, over medium-low heat until chocolate melts and mixture is smooth. Remove from heat; stir in pecans, vanilla, and salt. Stir in cookies. Spread fudge into prepared dish. Let stand 4 hours or until firm. Remove fudge in foil onto a cutting board; peel away foil, and cut fudge into squares. **Yield: 2¼ lb.**

Apricot-and-Strawberry Chèvre

editor's favorite • gift idea • make ahead

Apricot-and-Strawberry Chèvre

Prep: 17 min.   Cook: 3 min.   Other: 2 hr., 5 min.

½	cup dried strawberries, chopped
½	cup dried apricots, chopped
4	oz. chèvre (goat cheese)
1	(3-oz.) package cream cheese, softened
2	Tbsp. finely chopped red onion
2	Tbsp. apple cider vinegar
1½	tsp. chopped fresh rosemary
⅛	tsp. freshly ground pepper
Gingersnaps	

Bring strawberries, apricots, and water to cover to a boil in a small saucepan. Remove from heat; cover and let stand 5 minutes. Drain and let cool completely.

Process goat cheese and next 5 ingredients in a food processor until combined. Stir in chopped fruit by hand.

Shape cheese mixture into a 12" log; cut log into 3 (4") logs. Wrap each log in plastic wrap, and chill at least 2 hours. Serve with gingersnaps. Store cheese logs in refrigerator up to 1 week. **Yield: 3 (4") logs.**

Stained Glass Christmas Trees

Multicolored sanding sugar makes these tasty trees look as if they've been trimmed in holiday lights.

Prep: 23 min.   Cook: 18 min.   Other: 1 hr., 30 min.

1	cup unsalted butter, softened
½	cup powdered sugar
1	tsp. lemon zest
1	Tbsp. vanilla bean paste
¼	tsp. almond extract
2¼	cups all-purpose flour
½	tsp. salt
	Parchment paper
1	egg white, lightly beaten
1	(5-oz.) jar multicolored sanding sugar (we tested with Williams-Sonoma decorating sugar)

Beat butter at medium speed with an electric mixer until creamy. Gradually add powdered sugar, beating until smooth. Add lemon zest, vanilla bean paste, and almond extract, beating until blended.

Combine flour and salt; gradually add to butter mixture, beating just until blended. Shape dough into a ball, and divide in half. Flatten each half into a round disk; wrap each in plastic wrap, and chill at least 1 hour or until firm.

Preheat oven to 350°. Line 2 large baking sheets with parchment paper. Roll out dough, 1 portion at a time, to ¼" thickness on a floured surface. Cut into Christmas tree shapes using a 5½" Christmas tree cookie cutter. Place Christmas tree cutouts 1" apart on prepared baking sheets. Brush cookies with egg white, and sprinkle with multicolored sugar.

Bake at 350° for 18 minutes or until edges of cookies are lightly browned. Cool 5 minutes on baking sheets; remove cookies to wire racks to cool completely. **Yield: 14 cookies.**

Note: Other brands of decorating sugar would also work; the sugar might be finer in texture if using grocery store brands.

Cranberry-Pecan Coffee Cakes

These tender cranberry-and-nut streusel loaves are sure to please friends and neighbors.

Prep: 29 min.   Cook: 50 min.   Other: 45 min.

½	cup butter, softened
1	cup sugar
2	large eggs
2	cups all-purpose flour
2	tsp. baking powder
½	tsp. baking soda
½	tsp. salt
1	(8-oz.) container sour cream
1	tsp. almond extract
1	tsp. vanilla extract
1	(16-oz.) can whole-berry cranberry sauce, stirred
1	cup coarsely chopped pecans
	Almond Cream Glaze

Preheat oven to 350°. Beat butter at medium speed with an electric mixer until creamy. Gradually add sugar, beating well. Add eggs, 1 at a time, beating until blended after each addition.

Combine flour and next 3 ingredients. Add flour mixture to butter mixture alternately with sour cream, beginning and ending with flour mixture. Stir in extracts.

Spoon ½ cup batter into each of 4 greased and floured 5¾" x 3" mini loaf pans. Spoon 3 Tbsp. cranberry sauce over batter in each pan, and spread lightly to edges; sprinkle 2 Tbsp. pecans over cranberry sauce in each pan. Repeat layers in each pan using remaining batter, cranberry sauce, and pecans.

Bake at 350° for 48 to 50 minutes or until a wooden pick inserted in center comes out clean. Cool in pans on a wire rack 15 minutes; remove from pans, and let cool completely. Drizzle glaze over cooled cakes. **Yield: 4 mini coffee cakes.**

Almond Cream Glaze:

Prep: 6 min.

¾	cup powdered sugar
2	Tbsp. whipping cream
½	tsp. almond extract

Stir together all ingredients. **Yield: ⅓ cup.**

Chocolate Granola Brittle

The beauty of this recipe is that you can make a decadent brittle in the microwave in half the time it takes to make the traditional candy. If you want to make more than one pound, don't double the recipe—it won't give you the same result. Just make it twice.

Prep: 6 min.   Cook: 10 min.

Cranberry-Pecan Coffee Cakes

1   cup sugar
½   cup light corn syrup
⅛   tsp. salt
1   cup coarsely chopped pecans
1   Tbsp. butter
1   tsp. vanilla extract
1   tsp. baking soda
Parchment paper
¾   cup chocolate granola (we tested with
     Bear Naked chocolate granola)
3   (1-oz.) semisweet chocolate baking squares
1½   Tbsp. shortening

Combine first 3 ingredients in a 2-qt. glass bowl. Microwave at HIGH 5 minutes, using an 1100-watt microwave oven (add 1 more minute if using a 700-watt microwave oven). Stir in pecans. Microwave 1 minute, 30 seconds in an 1100-watt oven (add 1 more minute in 700-watt oven). Stir in butter and vanilla. Microwave 1 minute and 45 seconds in an 1100-watt oven (add 1 more minute in 700-watt oven) or until candy is the color of peanut butter. Stir in baking soda (mixture will bubble).

Quickly pour candy onto a lightly greased rimless baking sheet. (Pour as thinly as possible without spreading candy.) Cover brittle quickly with parchment paper, and use a rolling pin to thin out candy; peel off parchment. Sprinkle granola over brittle. Replace parchment, and use rolling pin to adhere granola to brittle; peel off parchment. Cool brittle completely; break into desired-size pieces.

Melt semisweet chocolate squares and shortening in a small bowl in the microwave oven at HIGH, 1½ to 2 minutes, stirring after 1 minute. Dip each piece of brittle halfway into chocolate mixture. Place dipped brittle on parchment paper to harden. Store in an airtight container. **Yield: about 1 lb.**

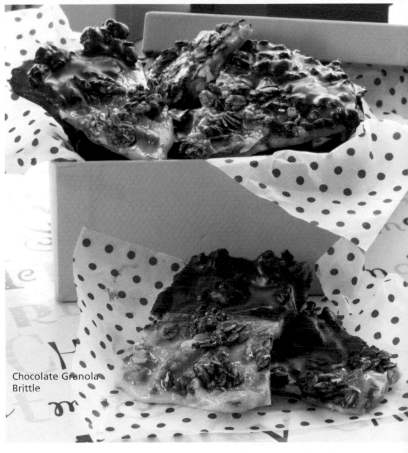

Chocolate Granola Brittle

editor's favorite • gift idea

Currant Shortbread

The marvelous features of this shortbread? It's wonderfully thick and not too sweet.

Prep: 8 min.   Cook: 37 min.   Other: 30 min.

Parchment paper
1	cup butter, softened
⅔	cup sugar
2¼	cups all-purpose flour
½	cup currants
1	tsp. orange zest
½	tsp. salt
¾	tsp. ground cardamom (optional)
1	Tbsp. sugar

Preheat oven to 325°. Line a large baking sheet with parchment paper, and set aside.

Beat butter and ⅔ cup sugar in a large mixing bowl at medium speed with an electric mixer 1 minute or until light and fluffy. Add flour, next 3 ingredients, and, if desired, cardamom to butter mixture. Beat at low speed until a dough forms.

Shape dough into a ball, and place on prepared baking sheet. Pat dough into an 8" circle. Using a sharp knife, cut dough into 12 wedges. (Do not separate wedges.) Sprinkle dough with 1 Tbsp. sugar.

Bake at 325° for 35 to 37 minutes or until golden. Remove shortbread to a wire rack, and cool completely. Cut into wedges. **Yield: 1 dozen.**

Red Velvet Swirl Pound Cake

Old-fashioned pound cake goes uptown with a red velvet swirl, thick white glaze, and sparkling glitter. (shown on cover)

Prep: 19 min.   Cook: 1 hr., 5 min.   Other: 1 hr., 35 min.

3	cups sifted cake flour
¾	tsp. salt
1	cup unsalted butter, softened
3	cups granulated sugar
6	large eggs
1	cup whipping cream
1	Tbsp. vanilla extract
½	tsp. almond extract
⅓	cup milk chocolate morsels, melted (we tested with Hershey's)
1¼	tsp. red liquid food coloring
3	cups powdered sugar
9	Tbsp. whipping cream

Pinch of salt
Edible white glitter

Preheat oven to 350°. Sift together flour and ¾ tsp. salt in a bowl.

Beat butter in a large mixing bowl at medium speed with an electric mixer 2 minutes or until creamy. Gradually add granulated sugar; beat at medium speed 5 minutes or until light and fluffy. Add eggs, 1 at a time, beating just until yellow disappears.

Gradually add one half of flour mixture to butter mixture, beating at low speed. Add 1 cup cream and extracts, beating just until blended. Add remaining flour mixture, beating just until blended. Scrape down sides of bowl; increase speed to medium-high and beat 5 minutes. (Batter will become very creamy and satiny).

Reserve 1½ cups batter. Pour remaining batter into a greased and floured 10" tube pan. Add melted chocolate and food coloring to reserved batter; stir until blended. Add to batter in pan in 2 batches, using a spoon to swirl the batters.

Bake at 350° for 1 hour and 5 minutes or until a long wooden pick inserted in center comes out clean. Cool in pan on a wire rack 30 minutes. Run a knife around edges to loosen cake; cool completely in pan.

Whisk together powdered sugar, 9 Tbsp. cream, and pinch of salt in a bowl until smooth; spoon thickly over cake. Let stand 5 minutes; sprinkle with glitter. **Yield: 12 servings.**

Caramel-Pecan Popcorn Crunch

These crisp, buttery popcorn clusters with toasted pecans rival any sweet popcorn snack you can buy at the store. (shown on page 160)

Prep: 5 min.   Cook: 1 hr., 50 min.   Other: 30 min.

2	cups pecan halves
2	(3.5-oz.) packages natural-flavored microwave popcorn, popped (we tested with Newman's Own)
2	cups firmly packed light brown sugar
½	cup unsalted butter
½	cup light corn syrup
2	tsp. vanilla extract
½	tsp. almond extract
½	tsp. salt
½	tsp. baking soda

Preheat oven to 350°. Bake pecans in a single layer in a shallow pan 8 to 10 minutes or until lightly toasted and fragrant.

Reduce oven temperature to 250°. Combine popcorn and pecans in a lightly greased 16" x 12" x 3" roasting pan.

Combine brown sugar, butter, and corn syrup in a 2½-qt. heavy saucepan. Bring to a boil over medium-high heat, stirring until butter melts. Wash down sides of pan with a brush dipped in hot water. Insert a candy thermometer into brown sugar mixture. Cook until thermometer registers 256° (hard ball stage), about 4 minutes. (Do not stir.)

Remove from heat; stir in extracts, salt, and soda. Gradually pour brown sugar mixture over popcorn and nuts, stirring gently to coat well, using a long-handled spoon.

Bake at 250° for 1½ hours or until dry, stirring occasionally. Cool completely in pan. Break into clusters, and store in an airtight container up to 2 weeks. **Yield: 25 cups.**

Note: It's often more economical to buy packaged popcorn kernels than microwave popcorn. Use ⅔ cup unpopped popcorn kernels for this recipe. Pop kernels according to package directions.

Recipe on page 159

caramel · pecan popcorn crunch

caramel · pecan popcorn crunch

caramel · pecan popcorn crunch

Toffee Peanuts

Packaging Nutty Gifts

Pack these crunchy recipes in cellophane bags; then give gift baskets, each containing a bag of all four treats.

Praline Pecans

Sweet Rosemary Mixed Nuts

Praline Pecans

These cinnamon-sugared nuts make a great salad topper.
Try them chilled, too, as a munchie with yogurt.

Prep: 6 min.   Cook: 20 min.   Other: 30 min.

4½   cups pecan halves (1 lb.)
1   cup firmly packed light brown sugar
⅓   cup butter
¼   tsp. ground cinnamon
½   tsp. salt
1   Tbsp. vanilla bean paste or vanilla extract

Preheat oven to 350°. Bake pecans in a single layer in a shallow pan 8 to 10 minutes or until toasted and fragrant.

Lay two 12" sheets of aluminum foil side by side lengthwise. Coat foil with cooking spray.

Combine sugar and next 4 ingredients in a large non-stick skillet over medium heat; cook 4 minutes or until bubbly. Stir in pecans; cook, stirring constantly, 6 minutes.

Pour pecans onto prepared foil. Gently separate pecans using 2 forks. Cool completely. Store pecans in an airtight container or zip-top plastic bag at room temperature or in refrigerator up to 1 week. **Yield: 5 cups.**

Note: Find vanilla bean paste at a gourmet cook store.

Toffee Peanuts

Use this recipe method to candy-coat any mix of nuts, such as blanched almonds, whole cashews, walnut halves, or a combination of the three.

Prep: 5 min.   Cook: 27 min.   Other: 30 min.

1½   cups sugar
¼   cup butter
4   cups shelled raw peanuts
½   tsp. salt
¼   tsp. ground cinnamon

Lightly grease a large rimmed baking sheet; set aside.

Stir together sugar, butter, and ½ cup water in a large deep skillet over medium heat; cook, stirring constantly, 3 minutes or until butter melts and sugar dissolves.

Increase heat to medium-high; add peanuts, and cook, stirring often, 15 minutes or until mixture becomes dry. Reduce heat to medium, and continue to cook 6 to 9 minutes, stirring often, until sugar melts, is golden, and coats nuts. (Do not stir constantly.) Sprinkle with salt and cinnamon; stir well. Spread nuts in a single layer on prepared baking sheet. Cool completely; break nuts apart. Store in an airtight container up to 2 weeks. **Yield: 7 cups.**

Sweet Rosemary Mixed Nuts

These fragrant nuts are ideal for serving alongside cocktails or hors d'oeuvres at a holiday party.

Prep: 7 min.   Cook: 15 min.   Other: 30 min.

2   cups walnut halves
1   cup raw blanched peanuts
1   cup whole almonds
1   cup whole cashews
¼   cup firmly packed dark brown sugar
2   Tbsp. chopped fresh rosemary
2   Tbsp. extra virgin olive oil
½   tsp. salt
½   tsp. dried crushed red pepper (optional)

Preheat oven to 350°. Combine first 8 ingredients and, if desired, red pepper in a large bowl, tossing to coat. Arrange nuts in a single layer on a large rimmed baking sheet.

Bake at 350° for 15 minutes or until toasted and fragrant, stirring twice. Cool completely. Store nuts at room temperature in an airtight container up to 2 weeks. **Yield: 5 cups.**

Homemade Graham
Crackers

Miniature Dried
Cherry-and-Almond
Scones

editor's favorite • gift idea

Homemade Graham Crackers

*For that extraspecial someone, include jumbo marshmallows
and a dark chocolate bar as a gift, turning these honey-infused
treats into the makings of gourmet s'mores.*

Prep: 26 min.   Cook: 20 min.   Other: 30 min.

Parchment paper
1   cup butter, softened
½   cup firmly packed dark brown sugar
2   Tbsp. honey
2   tsp. vanilla extract
1½   cups all-purpose flour
1   cup whole wheat pastry flour
2   tsp. ground cinnamon, divided
¾   tsp. baking soda
½   tsp. salt
3   Tbsp. granulated sugar

Preheat oven to 350°. Line a 17" x 12" jelly-roll pan
with parchment paper.

Beat butter and next 3 ingredients at medium speed
with an electric mixer 1 minute or until fluffy.

Combine flours, 1½ tsp. cinnamon, baking soda, and
salt in a large bowl; add to butter mixture, beating just
until blended.

Use dampened fingertips to press dough into prepared
pan. Cover dough with parchment paper; smooth surface
of dough with bottom of a dry measuring cup. Remove
and discard parchment paper. Combine remaining ½ tsp.
cinnamon and 3 Tbsp. granulated sugar in a small bowl;
sprinkle over dough. Using tines of a fork, score dough
into 24 squares, pressing completely through dough with
each indentation.

Bake at 350° for 20 minutes or until browned and crisp.
While crackers are still warm, score again. Cool completely
in pan on a wire rack; break into individual crackers.
Yield: 2 dozen.

Miniature Dried Cherry-and-Almond Scones

For an added touch, include a jar of jam with this bakery treat.

Prep: 15 min.   Cook: 15 min.

2¼ cups all-purpose flour
½   cup sugar, divided
1   Tbsp. baking powder
½   tsp. baking soda
½   tsp. salt
6   Tbsp. cold unsalted butter, cut into pieces
1   cup dried cherries
½   cup chopped toasted almonds
⅔   cup buttermilk
2   large eggs
¼   tsp. almond extract
Parchment paper

Preheat oven to 400°. Stir together flour, ¼ cup sugar, and next 3 ingredients in a large bowl; cut in butter with a pastry blender or fork until crumbly. Stir in cherries and almonds.

Whisk together buttermilk, 1 egg, and almond extract; add to flour mixture, stirring with a fork just until dry ingredients are moistened and mixture forms a shaggy dough.

Use floured hands to pat dough into a ½"-thick, 10" x 7" rectangle on a lightly floured surface; cut into 16 rectangles. Place scone dough on a parchment paper–lined baking sheet. Whisk together remaining egg and 1 tsp. water. Brush scones with egg wash; sprinkle with remaining ¼ cup sugar.

Bake at 400° for 12 to 15 minutes or until golden. **Yield: 16 scones.**

Grapefruit Marmalade

Prep: 25 min.   Cook: 37 min.   Other: 1 wk.

2   large ruby red grapefruit
1   lemon
⅛   tsp. baking soda
1   (1.75-oz.) package powdered pectin
    (we tested with SURE-JELL)
4   cups sugar

Scrub and rinse fruit well. Carefully remove rind from grapefruit and lemon with a vegetable peeler; coarsely chop rind to measure 1 cup. Place rind, 2½ cups water, and baking soda in a Dutch oven. Bring to a boil over high heat; cover, reduce heat, and simmer, stirring occasionally, 20 minutes.

While rind simmers, remove and discard white pith from grapefruit and lemon; cut fruit into ½"-thick slices. Remove seeds, and coarsely chop fruit to measure 2 cups fruit and juices.

Add fruit and juices to cooked rind. Bring to a boil; reduce heat and simmer, uncovered, 10 minutes. Stir in pectin. Bring to a rolling boil that cannot be stirred down; stir in sugar. Return to a rolling boil; boil 1 minute. Remove from heat; skim off any foam. Ladle into hot, sterilized jars, filling to within ⅛" of top. Seal jars. Cool completely. Store in refrigerator 1 week or until set before serving. Store up to 3 weeks in refrigerator. **Yield: 6 (½-pt.) jars.**

Poached Figs and Apricots

This poached fruit is perfect for spooning over roasted pork loin or grilled chicken. Or serve it over ice cream for dessert.

Prep: 14 min.   Cook: 50 min.   Other: 8 hr.

12 green cardamom pods
1   small lemon
1½ cups sugar
¼   cup apple cider vinegar
1   Tbsp. whole cloves
1   tsp. whole black peppercorns
4   (4") cinnamon sticks
1   (2") piece fresh ginger, peeled and thinly sliced
2   cups small dried figs
2   cups dried apricots

Tap cardamom pods gently with flat side of a meat mallet just until pods open slightly. Trim ends from lemon, and cut lemon into thin slices.

Bring cardamom, lemon slices, sugar, next 5 ingredients, and 5 cups water to a boil in a Dutch oven over medium-high heat, stirring often. Add figs and apricots; cover, reduce heat to medium-low, and cook 45 minutes or until fruit is tender.

Ladle fruit and liquid into hot, sterilized pint jars, filling to ⅛" of top. Seal jars, and cool completely. Chill at least 8 hours. Store in refrigerator up to 2 weeks. **Yield: 4 pints.**

GIFTS FROM *the Heart*

Handmade gifts are always appreciated. Whether it's a fun pillow stitched up in someone's favorite colors or a do-it-yourself gift tag for a wine bottle, the presents on these pages are as much fun to make as they are to receive.

Soft & Cuddly

Sew a pillow for someone special using scraps and remnants of fabrics and trims. The pillow shown here is backed with inexpensive felt that's cut along the edges to form a simple blocky trim. Select fabrics in coordinating hues for the pillow front. To create your own design, cut the desired shapes from fabric. Sew the shapes to a larger piece of fabric using a zigzag stitch. The zigzag stitch adds a casual look and also keeps the fabric edges from raveling. Sew trim around the outside edges of the pillow as you stitch the front and back pieces together, if you like, or leave it plain. That's the beauty of this design—it's as flexible as your own imagination!

Christmas Crafts

Break out the scissors and glue to show family and friends your artistic side. Gather materials such as felt, narrow ribbons and rickrack, sequins, buttons, and scrapbooking papers.

For gift card holders (opposite page), cut two pieces of felt large enough to hold a gift card. Glue or stitch the pieces together along the sides, leaving the top open. Decorate the holder with felt cutouts, buttons, and trims.

For treat bags (top left), cut two rectangles from felt for the bag front and back. Cut another long rectangle to form the sides and bottom. Sew the front and back pieces to the long rectangle to make a bag. Stitch on simple felt cutouts, if desired.

For bottle tags (top right), cut a rectangle from decorative paper, and cut a hole near the top of the rectangle to fit over the bottle neck. Glue or tie a personalized greeting to the larger tag.

For a magnetic greeting card (left), trim decorative paper to fit a standard photo mat, and glue in place. Add embellishments, as desired. Tape a family photo in place, and back the mat with magnetic strips.

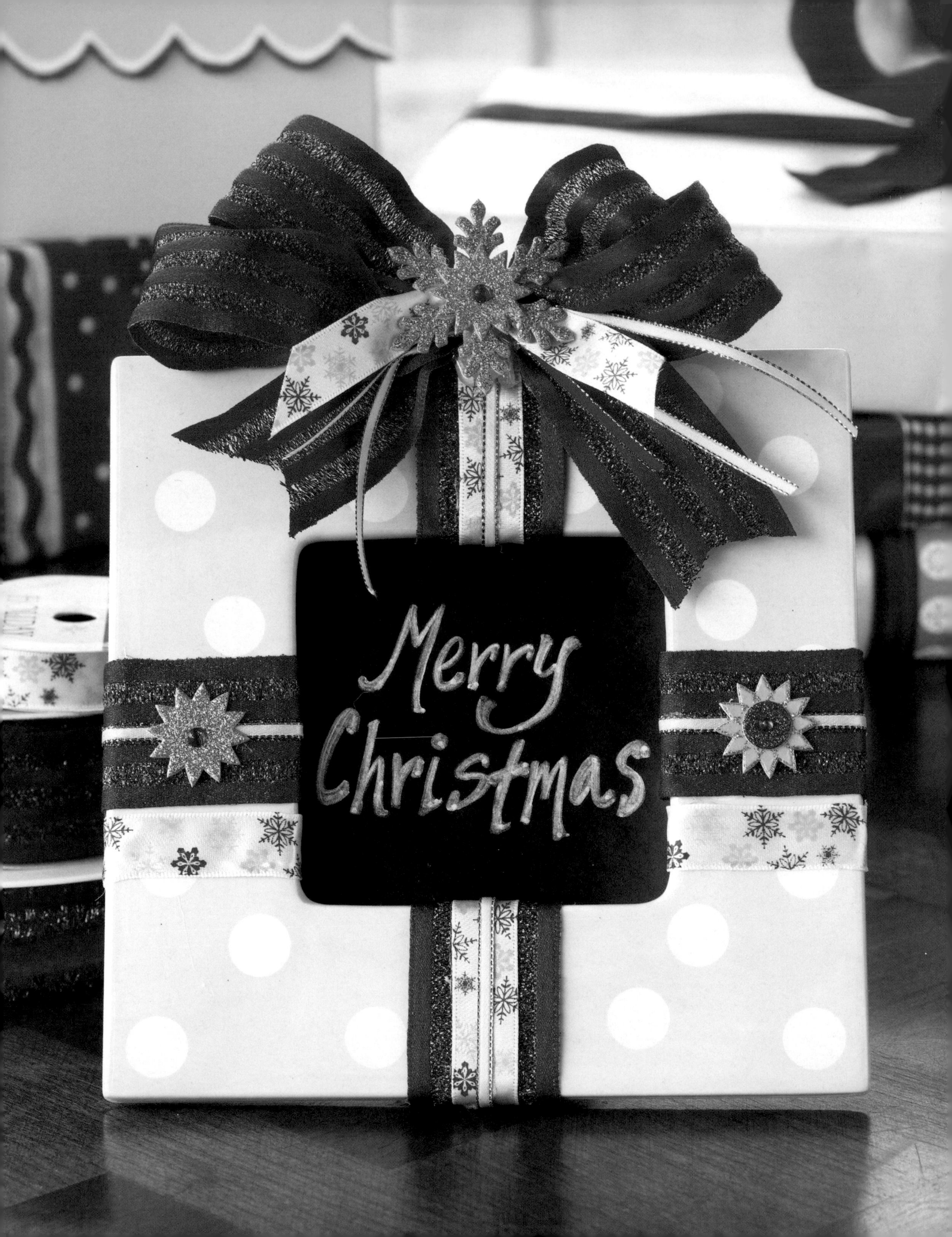
Merry Christmas

Framing to Please

Personalize plain picture frames for gifts that will be treasured as much for their creative flair as for their thoughtfulness. Suit the embellishments to the photo with such add-ons as holiday trims for a seasonal greeting, fishing tackle for a rustic look, kitchen utensils to frame a special recipe, or a handwritten phrase or verse to complement a family portrait.

WHERE TO *Find It*

Source information is current at the time of publication; however, we cannot guarantee availability of items. If an item is not listed, its source is unknown.

• pages 10-11—**votives:** HomArt, (888) 346-6278, www.homart.com; **pitcher:** Lamb's Ears, Ltd., Birmingham, AL, (205) 969-3138; **baker:** Revol, (888) 337-3865, www.revol-usa.com; **tray, square bowl, table runner:** Table Matters, Birmingham, AL, (205) 879-0125, www.table-matters.com; **serving stand:** Mary Carol Home Collection by The Gerson Companies, (800) 444-8172, www.gersoncompany.com

• page 14—**baker:** Revol, (888) 337-3865, www.revol-usa.com

• page 15—**bowl:** Table Matters, Birmingham, AL, (205) 879-0125, www.table-matters.com

• page 19—**pedestal:** HomArt, (888) 346-6278, www.homart.com; **shot glasses:** World Market, (877) 967-5362, www.worldmarket.com; Target, (800) 591-3869, www.target.com (Look for inexpensive 2-oz. shot glasses in restaurant-supply stores also)

• page 21—**lanterns, candles:** Pottery Barn, (888) 779-5176, www.potterybarn.com; **moss:** Michaels, (800) 642-4235, www.michaels.com

• page 25—**fabric (inset):** Amy Butler, Lotus Collection, Green Wallflower, by Westminster Rowan, (740) 587-2841, www.amybutlerdesign.com

• pages 26-27—**plates, mugs, jar with lid:** *Southern Living At HOME®*, www.southernlivingathome.com for ordering information; **snow village:** Lamb's Ears, Ltd., Birmingham, AL, (205) 969-3138

• page 28—**cake stands:** HomeGoods, (800) 614-HOME, www.homegoods.com

• page 29—**platter, plate in tray:** Tricia's Treasures, Birmingham, AL, (205) 871-9779; **wreath plate, tray:** Mary Carol Home Collection by The Gerson Companies, (800) 444-8172, www.gersoncompany.com

• page 30—**pedestal:** Crate & Barrel, (800) 967-6696, www.crateandbarrel.com; **elves:** Belk, (866) 235-5443, www.Belk.com; **table, chairs:** Pottery Barn Kids, (800) 993-4923, www.potterybarnkids.com; **elf stockings, candy cane scoops:** Swoozie's, (866) 796-6943, www.swoozies.com

• page 33—**candy cane bowl and saucer:** Swoozie's, (866) 796-6943, www.swoozies.com; **plate:** Crate & Barrel, (800) 967-6696, www.crateandbarrel.com

• page 35—**elf stocking:** Swoozie's, (866) 796-6943, www.swoozies.com; **jelly bean jar:** Michaels, (800) 642-4235, www.michaels.com; **peppermint pedestal:** Smith's Variety, Birmingham, AL, (205) 871-0841

• page 36—**cups:** Target, (800) 591-3869, www.target.com; **pedestal:** A'Mano, Birmingham, AL, (205) 871-9093, www.amanogifts.com

• pages 38-39—**linens, wooden charger platter:** Table Matters, Birmingham, AL, (205) 879-0125, www.table-matters.com

• page 42—**mugs, linens:** Table Matters, Birmingham, AL, (205) 879-0125, www.table-matters.com

• page 44—**ornament candleholders:** HomArt, (888) 346-6278, www.homart.com; **chargers, glasses:** *Southern Living At HOME®*, www.southernlivingathome.com for

ordering information; **linens (placemats, napkins):** Lamb's Ears, Ltd., Birmingham, AL, (205) 969-3138; **plates:** Mary Carol Home Collection by The Gerson Companies, (800) 444-8172, www.gersoncompany.com

• page 45—**tray:** Mary Carol Home Collection by The Gerson Companies, (800) 444-8172, www.gersoncompany.com; **glasses:** World Market, (877) 967-5362, www.worldmarket.com

• page 50—**china pattern:** Bromberg & Co., Inc., (205) 871-3276, www.brombergs.com

• page 51—**ornament candleholders:** HomArt, (888) 346-6278, www.homart.com; **napkin rings:** Table Matters, Birmingham, AL, (205) 879-0125, www.table-matters.com; **menu board and stand:** *Southern Living At HOME®*, www.southernlivingathome.com for ordering information

• page 52—**table runner:** Libeco, www.libeco.com; **dinnerware:** A'Mano, Birmingham, AL, (205) 871-9093, www.amanogifts.com

• page 53—**marble grapes:** Henhouse Antiques, Birmingham, AL, (205) 918-0505, www.shophenhouseantiques.com

• pages 54-55—**wine bottle candelabra:** www.sundancecatalog.com; **table runner, glass wine bottle holders, bowls:** Pottery Barn, (888) 779-5176, www.potterybarn.com; **ivory plates:** Mariposa, (800) 788-1304, www.mariposa-gift.com

• pages 56-57: **linens, placemats:** Art Home Furnishings, Birmingham, AL, (205) 879-3510

• pages 58-59—**domes:** Henhouse Antiques, Birmingham, AL, (205) 918-0505, www.shophenhouseantiques.com; Smith and Hawken, (800) 940-1170, www.smithandhawken.com; Pottery Barn, (888) 779-5176, www.potterybarn.com; *Southern Living At HOME®*, www.southernlivingathome.com for ordering information; **red table runner:** Pottery Barn, (888) 779-5176, www.potterybarn.com

• page 61—**plates, glassware, napkins, napkin rings:** Lamb's Ears, Ltd., Birmingham, AL, (205) 969-3138

• page 62—**butterflies:** Pottery Barn, (888) 779-5176, www.potterybarn.com; **large and small lanterns:** World Market, (877) 967-5362, www.worldmarket.com

• page 63—**takeout boxes:** Smith's Variety, Birmingham, AL, (205) 871-0841; **plates, charger:** Pottery Barn, (888) 779-5176, www.potterybarn.com

• page 65—**wreath plate:** Mary Carol Home Collection by The Gerson Companies, (800) 444-8172, www.gersoncompany.com

• page 66—**linens, placemats, moss spheres:** Table Matters, Birmingham, AL, (205) 879-0125, www.table-matters.com; **Christmas tree dinnerware:** Spode, Macys.com/Spode

• page 67—**coffee cup candle holders:** HomArt, (888) 346-6278, www.homart.com

• page 72—**metal trees, wreath, ribbon:** Flowerbuds, Inc., Birmingham, AL, (205) 822-5838

• page 74—**galvanized luminaries, galvanized star:** Smith and Hawken, (800) 940-1170, www.smithandhawken.com

• page 75—**wellies ornament:** Smith and Hawken, (800) 940-1170, www.smithandhawken.com

• page 77—**red lantern:** Jeremie, (404) 875-3593, www.jeremiecorp.com;

dk metal lanterns: Pottery Barn, (888) 779-5176, www.potterybarn.com

• pages 78-79—**bells:** Leaf & Petal, Birmingham, AL (205) 871-3832, www.leafnpetal.com

• page 81—**iron door-hanging plant container:** *Southern Living At HOME®*, www.southernlivingathome.com for ordering information; **red pot, tree candle, glass hurricane:** Smith and Hawken, (800) 940-1170, www.smithandhawken.com

• page 84—**silver pine cones, stockings, candles, ornaments, mercury glass container:** Pottery Barn, (888) 779-5176, www.potterybarn.com

• page 85—**tree:** Henhouse Antiques, Birmingham, AL, (205) 918-0505, www.shophenhouseantiques.com

• page 87—**stockings (Joy, brown and white), transferware china:** Mulberry Heights Antiques, Birmingham, AL, (205) 870-1300; **stocking holder frames:** Pottery Barn, (888) 779-5176, www.potterybarn.com

• pages 92-93—**Christmas fairies, jingle-bell garlands, glitter tree:** Flowerbuds, Inc., Birmingham, AL, (205) 822-5838; **firescreen:** *Southern Living At HOME®*, www.southernlivingathome.com for ordering information

• page 93—**stocking patterns:** Elf Stitchettes by Hillary Lang, © 2006 Wee Wonderfuls™, all rights reserved, www.weewonderfuls.com

• page 95—**Santas:** Lamb's Ears, Ltd., Birmingham, AL, (205) 969-3138

• pages 96-97—**glass bottles:** Hanna Antiques Mall, Birmingham, AL, (205) 323-6036; **globes:** HomArt, (888) 346-6278, www.homart.com

• page 98—**red bowl:** *Southern Living At HOME®*, www.southernlivingathome.com for ordering information

• page 99—**kitchen equipment and tools:** Williams-Sonoma, (877) 812-6235, www.williams-sonoma.com

• pages 102-103—**ladle candle holders (2nd & 4th on mantel):** Williams-Sonoma, (877) 812-6235, www.williams-sonoma.com; **ladle candle holder (upper right inset):** Hanna Antiques Mall, Birmingham, AL, (205) 323-6036

• page 112—**garland:** Christmas & Co., Birmingham, AL, (205) 823-6640

• page 118—**antique glass cake pedestal:** Attic Antiques, Birmingham, AL, (205) 991-6887

• page 126—**linen, cake pedestal:** Table Matters, Birmingham, AL, (205) 879-0125, www.table-matters.com

• page 129—**cupcake picks:** Michaels, (800) 642-4235, www.michaels.com

• page 134—**large lantern:** *Southern Living At HOME®*, www.southernlivingathome.com for ordering information

• page 140—**casserole dish, linen towel:** Table Matters, Birmingham, AL, (205) 879-0125, www.table-matters.com

• page 143—**casserole dish:** Revol, (888) 337-3865, www.revol-usa.com; **spoon:** Table Matters, Birmingham, AL, (205) 879-0125, www.table-matters.com

• page 146—**dish:** Table Matters, Birmingham, AL, (205) 879-0125, www.table-matters.com; **linen:** Pottery Barn, (888) 779-5176, www.potterybarn.com

• page 150—**linen:** Table Matters, Birmingham, AL, (205) 879-0125, www.table-matters.com

• page 160—**tiny green star ornaments:** Smith and Hawken, (800) 940-1170, www.smithandhawken.com

• page 169—**words on photo mat:** from "Let There Be Peace on Earth," by Sy Miller and Jill Jackson

RECINE *Index*

RECIPE *Index*

THANKS TO THESE *Contributors*

Editorial contributors

Rex Bowman	Kappi Hamilton
Stephanie Brennan	Hillary Lang
Lauren Brooks	Rebecca Lang
Lorrie Corvin	Alison Lewis
Adrienne Davis	Debby Maugans
Georgia Downard	Jackie Mills
Anna Gilmore	Liz Pearson
Caroline Grant	

Thanks to the following homeowners

Kimber and Jim Bathie	Buffy and Zeb Hargett
Donna Beauchamp	Judy and Bert Hill
Nancy and Buck Brock	Janet and Stoney Jackson
Kacy Carroll	Cindy Matthews
Kay Clarke	Leslie Naff
Taryn Drennen	Josephine and Paul Pankey
Christina L. Eckert	Leslie and John Simpson
William Hamilton	Anne and Steve Varner

Thanks to these Birmingham businesses

A'Mano	Lamb's Ears, Ltd.
Bromberg & Co., Inc.	Leaf & Petal
Christine's	Mulberry Heights Antiques
Christmas & Co.	Pottery Barn
Davis Wholesale Flowers	Table Matters
Flowerbuds, Inc.	Tricia's Treasures
Henhouse Antiques	

USE THIS HANDY PLANNING SECTION TO BE ORGANIZED AND READY
FOR FUN WHEN THE HOLIDAY SEASON ARRIVES. IT'S ALSO A USEFUL
REFERENCE WHEN YOU START MAKING PLANS FOR CHRISTMAS 2010!

Holiday Planner

NOVEMBER *2009*

Sunday	Monday	Tuesday	Wednesday
1	2	3	4
8	9	10	11
15	16	17	18
22	23	24	25
29	30		

Thursday	Friday	Saturday
5	6	7
12	13	14
19	20	21
Thanksgiving 26	27	28

Holiday-Ready Pantry

Be prepared for seasonal cooking and baking by stocking up on these items.

- ☐ Assorted coffees, teas, hot chocolate, and eggnog
- ☐ Wine, beer, and soft drinks
- ☐ White, brown, and powdered sugars
- ☐ Ground allspice, cinnamon, cloves, ginger, and nutmeg
- ☐ Baking soda and baking powder
- ☐ Seasonal fresh herbs
- ☐ Baking chocolate
- ☐ Semisweet chocolate morsels
- ☐ Assorted nuts
- ☐ Flaked coconut
- ☐ Sweetened condensed milk and evaporated milk
- ☐ Whipping cream
- ☐ Jams, jellies, and preserves
- ☐ Raisins, cranberries, and other fresh or dried fruits
- ☐ Canned pumpkin
- ☐ Frozen/refrigerated bread dough, biscuits, and croissants

Things to do

DECEMBER *2009*

Sunday	Monday	Tuesday	Wednesday
		1	2
6	7	8	9
13	14	15	16
20	21	22	23
27	28	29	30

Thursday	Friday	Saturday
3	*4*	*5*
10	*11*	*12*
17	*18*	*19*
Christmas Eve *24*	Christmas *25*	*26*
New Year's Eve *31*		

Guest-ready Checklist

Impress holiday houseguests with these thoughtful gestures that will make even a den with a sofa bed seem like an upscale hotel room.

- Lavish with luxuries. Dress the bed with high-quality sheets and plump pillows. Have extra blankets readily available. Provide guests with a luggage stand, or clear space in the closet for their things.
- Create a "scentsational" ambience. Arrange a selection of scented lotions and a candle on a tray in the bedroom. Guests will appreciate a soothing lotion after a day out and about in brisk winter weather, and a fresh-scented candle will assure a calm prelude to a long winter's nap.
- Offer good, short reads. Stack volumes of short stories, poetry, or light-hearted essays on the nightstand for relaxing bedtime reading.
- Plug in soothing sounds. Place a sound machine in the room to fill it with the peaceful lull of nature sounds, such as a babbling brook or sweet birdsong, and to drown out household hubbub. Some alarm clocks have this feature, or look for inexpensive sound machines at discount centers.
- Fashion a mini-spa. In the bathroom, organize bars of soap and small bottles of shampoo and shower gel in clear apothecary jars. Provide plenty of hand towels, washcloths, and bath towels in a pretty basket.

Decorating PLANNER

Use these lines to list what you'll need for seasonal decorations all through the house.

Decorative materials needed

from the yard ....

....

from around the house ....

....

from the store ....

....

other ....

Holiday decorations

for the table ....

....

for the door..

....

for the mantel ....

....

for the staircase..

....

other ....

Simple Tips for a Living Christmas Tree

Selecting a living Christmas tree double bonus: You can decorate and enjoy the tree indoors, and after the holidays, you can plant it outside to appreciate for years to come. Before heading to the nursery or tree lot, here are a few considerations.

• Choose a tree that's right for your climate and your yard. Consider the tree's mature size, and make sure the planting area you select provides plenty of room for the tree to grow. Most conifers prefer full sun; be sure to check your tree's specific requirements.

• Price will be determined by the species, size, and shearing done by the grower. Conifers that are sheared and tapered cost more than landscape-grade trees that receive no special care. Living Christmas trees can range from $30 to more than $300.

• Trees are sold container-grown or balled-and-burlapped (B&B). Trees in containers weigh less and don't require potting indoors, while the larger B&B trees adapt easily once planted. Unless you want a really large tree, go with a container-grown one.

• When you bring your tree home, choose a decorative container (a must for a B&B tree, optional for a tree already in a container).

Select one close to the size of the root-ball to maintain moisture levels. Fill in any gaps with potting soil.

• Place the tree away from direct heat sources, including vents, fireplaces, and kitchen stoves. A cool room (especially one with lots of natural light) is best so the tree doesn't break dormancy. Keep the tree indoors for no more than 10 days.

• Water the tree daily by placing about 30 ice cubes onto the top of the root-ball and letting them melt slowly. Strings of lights emit heat that can cause trees to dry out quickly, so use them for short periods of time.

• To plant the tree, cut away nylon string from a B&B tree using a sharp knife if the neck of the root-ball has been bound; if the material covering the root-ball is nylon rather than organic material like burlap, carefully remove, as it will inhibit rooting. Lightly score the root-ball with a sharp knife. Plant so the root-ball is 1 to 2 inches above ground level. Where soils are heavy and clay-based, plant even higher (3 to 4 inches above ground level). Water well at planting and regularly where winters are dry. Do not fertilize if planting in winter; instead, feed in early spring.

Mix-and-Match MENUS

Menus below are based on recipes in the book.

Holiday Dessert Party

Serves 18 to 24

Red Velvet Swirl Pound Cake (page 159)

Dark Chocolate-Toffee Brownie Shooters (page 18)

Oatmeal Turtle Bars (page 36)

Pumpkin Spice Bars (page 124)

Easy Chocolate Chip Cookie Fudge (page 155)

Praline Pecans (page 161)

Toffee Peanuts (page 161)

Açái-Berry Mulled Cider (page 12)

Coffee   Hot chocolate

❧

Harvest Fare

Serves 8

Whole Acorn Squash Cream Soup (2x) (page 150)

Sweet-and-Spicy Glazed Turkey [with roasted
Brussels sprouts] (page 135)

Mustardy Carrots With Lemon and Green Onions (page 148)

Pumpkin Spice Bars (page 124)

❧

Special Occasion Dinner

Serves 4

Roasted Lemon Chicken (page 136)

Hot rice

Asparagus With Gremolata (page 150)

Mini Chocolate-Cherry Layer Cakes (page 43)

Ladies Lunch

Serves 4

Fruit Skewers With Strawberry Dip (page 32)

Crispy Chicken Salad With Dried Cranberries,
Walnuts, and Blue Cheese (page 138)

Garlic breadsticks

Walnut Scotchies (page 113)

❧

Easy Party Plan

Serves 8

Blood Orange Martinis (page 12)

Fig, Prosciutto, and Blue Cheese Squares (page 14)

Party Paella Casserole (page 142)

Mixed greens salad

Crusty rolls

White Christmas Coconut Sheet Cake
(page 125)

❧

Mediterranean Night

Serves 6

Mediterranean Roasted Almonds (page 13)

Mediterranean Chicken Kebabs (page 144)

Tangy Cauliflower With Tomatoes, Olives,
and Feta (page 147)

Buttered green beans

Chocolate Cherry Galettes (page 128)

Party PLANNER

Make entertaining easy by using this planning chart to coordinate your party menu.

guests	what they're bringing	serving pieces needed
....	☐ appetizer ☐ beverage ☐ bread ☐ main dish ☐ side dish ☐ dessert	....
....	☐ appetizer ☐ beverage ☐ bread ☐ main dish ☐ side dish ☐ dessert	....
....	☐ appetizer ☐ beverage ☐ bread ☐ main dish ☐ side dish ☐ dessert	....
....	☐ appetizer ☐ beverage ☐ bread ☐ main dish ☐ side dish ☐ dessert	....
....	☐ appetizer ☐ beverage ☐ bread ☐ main dish ☐ side dish ☐ dessert	....
....	☐ appetizer ☐ beverage ☐ bread ☐ main dish ☐ side dish ☐ dessert	....
....	☐ appetizer ☐ beverage ☐ bread ☐ main dish ☐ side dish ☐ dessert	....
....	☐ appetizer ☐ beverage ☐ bread ☐ main dish ☐ side dish ☐ dessert	....
....	☐ appetizer ☐ beverage ☐ bread ☐ main dish ☐ side dish ☐ dessert	....
....	☐ appetizer ☐ beverage ☐ bread ☐ main dish ☐ side dish ☐ dessert	....
....	☐ appetizer ☐ beverage ☐ bread ☐ main dish ☐ side dish ☐ dessert	....
....	☐ appetizer ☐ beverage ☐ bread ☐ main dish ☐ side dish ☐ dessert	....
....	☐ appetizer ☐ beverage ☐ bread ☐ main dish ☐ side dish ☐ dessert	....
....	☐ appetizer ☐ beverage ☐ bread ☐ main dish ☐ side dish ☐ dessert	....
....	☐ appetizer ☐ beverage ☐ bread ☐ main dish ☐ side dish ☐ dessert	....
....		....

Party Guest List

Pantry List

Party To-Do List

Christmas Dinner PLANNER

Get a jump start on the big holiday meal by writing your menu, to-do list, and guest list on these pages.

Menu Ideas

....
....
....
....
....
....
....
....
....

Dinner To-Do List

....
....
....
....
....
....
....
....
....
....
....
....

Christmas Dinner Guest List

....
....
....
....
....
....
....
....
....
....
....
....
....
....

Bundt Offerings

Bundt cakes baked in decorative pans are festive additions to holiday meals, and make welcome gifts as well. You'll find baking instructions included on the packaging with most specialty pans, but because the same cake batter rises and bakes differently in each pan, keep these helpful tips in mind.

• It's important to fill pans with the correct amount of batter. If you use a smaller pan than is called for in a recipe, fill the pan no more than one-half to two-thirds full, and reduce the bake time. Too much batter will overflow and cause the cake to collapse back into the pan. Too little batter will leave the sides of the pan exposed and shield the cake from baking evenly.

• When baking more than one cake at a time, make sure pans are similar in size. If not, bake the larger cake first, and refrigerate any remaining batter up to 1½ hours. Return batter to room temperature before baking. Refrigeration slows the activation process of leavening, but a sudden burst of hot air from the oven will quickly collapse a cold batter.

• Even when using the same-size pans, bake times can vary according to the density of the batter. Depending on the recipe, a cake may take as little as 45 minutes or as long as 1½ hours to bake in a 12-cup Bundt pan.

• One Bundt cake recipe fills 6 to 8 small (5- x 3-inch) loaf pans and usually bakes in 30 to 40 minutes. Each pan holds a little over a cup of batter, leaving just the right amount of room to add a frosting or glaze and some fun toppings when cakes are cool. Larger (8- x 4-inch) loaf pans require 50 to 60 minutes of bake time.

The Easy Way Out

• To easily release cakes from shaped pans, grease all the flutes and crevices before adding batter to the pan. Use a pastry brush to generously coat the bottom and sides of the pan with a solid vegetable shortening such as Crisco. Lightly sprinkle with flour, tilting and tapping pans so flour completely covers greased surfaces; invert pans, and gently tap out any excess flour.

• Before removing cake from pan after baking, cool according to recipe directions. Invert pan over a wire rack, gently shaking pan to release cake. If needed, use the blade of a small icing spatula to loosen the sides of cake from pan.

• With smaller muffin pans and molds, you may find it easier to use a vegetable cooking spray with flour, such as PAM® Baking, Crisco® No-Stick Cooking Spray with Flour, or Baker's Joy® Original No-Stick Baking Spray with Flour.

Gifts AND *Greetings*

Keep a personalized record of sizes and gifts to use as a ready reference for gift-giving occasions year-round. Write names and addresses on the facing page, and you'll have mailing information close at hand.

Gift List and Size Charts

name /sizes	gift purchased/made	sent/delivered

name ....

jeans_____ shirt_____ sweater_____ jacket_____ shoes_____ belt_____

blouse_____ skirt_____ slacks_____ dress_____ suit_____ coat_____

pajamas_____ robe_____ hat_____ gloves_____ ring_____

name ....

jeans_____ shirt_____ sweater_____ jacket_____ shoes_____ belt_____

blouse_____ skirt_____ slacks_____ dress_____ suit_____ coat_____

pajamas_____ robe_____ hat_____ gloves_____ ring_____

name ....

jeans_____ shirt_____ sweater_____ jacket_____ shoes_____ belt_____

blouse_____ skirt_____ slacks_____ dress_____ suit_____ coat_____

pajamas_____ robe_____ hat_____ gloves_____ ring_____

name ....

jeans_____ shirt_____ sweater_____ jacket_____ shoes_____ belt_____

blouse_____ skirt_____ slacks_____ dress_____ suit_____ coat_____

pajamas_____ robe_____ hat_____ gloves_____ ring_____

name ....

jeans_____ shirt_____ sweater_____ jacket_____ shoes_____ belt_____

blouse_____ skirt_____ slacks_____ dress_____ suit_____ coat_____

pajamas_____ robe_____ hat_____ gloves_____ ring_____

name ....

jeans_____ shirt_____ sweater_____ jacket_____ shoes_____ belt_____

blouse_____ skirt_____ slacks_____ dress_____ suit_____ coat_____

pajamas_____ robe_____ hat_____ gloves_____ ring_____

name ....

jeans_____ shirt_____ sweater_____ jacket_____ shoes_____ belt_____

blouse_____ skirt_____ slacks_____ dress_____ suit_____ coat_____

pajamas_____ robe_____ hat_____ gloves_____ ring_____

Christmas Card List

name	address	sent/delivered

Holiday MEMORIES

Capture highlights of this year's best holiday moments here.

Treasured Traditions

Record your family's favorite holiday customs and pastimes on these lines.

....

....

....

....

....

....

....

....

....

....

....

....

....

Special Holiday Activities

Keep a list of the seasonal events you look forward to year after year.

....

....

....

....

....

....

....

....

....